Ten Great Hymn Writers

And Their Hymns

Peter Currie

TEN GREAT
HYMN WRITERS

AND THEIR HYMNS

PETER CURRIE

AMBASSADOR INTERNATIONAL
GREENVILLE, SOUTH CAROLINA & BELFAST, NORTHERN IRELAND

www.ambassador-international.com

TEN GREAT HYMN WRITERS AND THEIR HYMNS

©2025 by Peter Currie

All rights reserved

Hardcover ISBN: 978-1-64960-889-5
Paperback ISBN: 978-1-64960-502-3
eISBN: 978-1-64960-546-7

Cover design and Interior Typesetting by Karen Slayne

Edited by Katie Cruice Smith and Kimberly Davis

Scripture taken from the New King James Version®. Copyright © 1982 by Thomas Nelson. Used by permission. All rights reserved.

King David Playing the Harp by Gerard van Honthorst is in the public domain.

AMBASSADOR INTERNATIONAL
Emerald House Group, Incorporated
411 University Ridge, Suite B14
Greenville, SC 29601, USA
www.ambassador-international.com

AMBASSADOR BOOKS
The Mount
2 Woodstock Link
Belfast, BT6 8DD, Northern Ireland, UK
www.ambassadormedia.co.uk

The colophon is a trademark of Ambassador, a Christian publishing company.

This Book is Dedicated to
TEN GREAT HYMN WRITERS
WHO HAVE HELPED MANY PEOPLE,
INCLUDING MYSELF,
Sing Praises to The Lord.

&NDORSEMENTS

"This book introduces us to ten great hymn writers and some of their hymns that continue to be sung in many churches today. We glimpse into the backgrounds, lives, and, importantly, the hymn writers' trust in the Lord Jesus Christ. It references favorite tunes, preferred versions, and personal meaning from Peter, all of which make this an interesting and edifying read. However, to think that this was just a book about hymn writers, I believe, misses the heart of what makes this book meaningful.

The focus, as I see it, is not to glorify people from history and their poetic and musical skills but to glorify God and to point readers to the Lord Jesus Christ. People who love the Lord, as the hymn writers did, can be taken up with hymns of praise to Him; whereas Peter's desire for people who have not yet trusted Christ is that they would be captivated by the beauty of the Savior and turn to Him in repentance and faith."

—**Pastor Stuart Davis**
Trinity Road Chapel

&NDORSEMENTS
(cont.)

"I have often thought what an untapped, apologetic support for the genuineness of the Christian faith is found in the multiple thousands of Christian hymns composed over the centuries. The people of God simply cannot remain silent. God is that great! And He is that good! And those with requisite skill and creativity have expressed this greatness and goodness in hymns that extol our glorious God and His gracious salvation in Christ.

Peter Currie provides a window into some of the richness of this history as he explores ten of the most skillful, influential, and productive hymn writers of the English tradition. What a feast awaits those who explore these pages! One is reminded over and again of rich biblical and theological truths that are so precious, rich, stirring, and life-shaping that they simply must be sung! We owe a great debt of gratitude to these godly hymn writers and to our author for reminding us and for instructing us in ways that expose something of the brilliance of our God through the excellence of these hymnic expressions of His glory and praise."

—**Bruce A. Ware, Professor of Christian Theology**
Southern Seminary, Louisville, Kentucky, USA

Author's Note

The Bible commands Christians to speak "to one another in psalms and hymns and spiritual songs, singing and making melody in your heart to the Lord" (Eph. 5:19). The book of Psalms was the songbook of the Old Testament and should continue to be used, but New Testament Christians are encouraged to employ hymns and spiritual songs as well. Hymns and spiritual songs are distinct from one another in that hymns are spiritual songs that include direct ascription of praise to God. Although other spiritual songs may not include that direct ascription of praise, they remain valuable because they enable both teaching and admonishment when sung together as a congregation (Col. 3:16). That said, the terms *hymns* and *songs* appear interchangeably throughout this book.

For Spirit-filled believers, this exhortation is more description than command. Christians cannot help singing because "[the Lord] has put a new song in my mouth—Praise to our God" (Psalm 40:3). The "new song" does not mean that believers must sing modern works all the time; it refers to voicing the new song of redemption (Rev. 5:8-10) in addition to the old song of creation (Rev. 4:8-11). Furthermore, this counsel does not preclude solitary hymn-singing; the Bible encourages individual Christians to speak to themselves, a practice illustrated in Psalms 42 and 43.

Accomplishing this goal requires only suitable words and a congenial tune. The latter element is also important. For example, the tune "Love Unknown," written in 1925 by John Ireland, gave Samuel Crossman's great hymn mentioned below a new lease on life. At the end of this book, there is an appendix giving a suggested tune for every psalm and hymn mentioned.

Early centuries of the Christian era produced some hymns of great worth that continue to be published and sung in the modern day. The following list offers a few examples and print sources where they can be found:

- "O Jesus, Lord of Heavenly Grace" by Ambrose of Milan, fourth century (*Christian Hymns*, 2004)
- "The King Shall Come When Morning Dawns" from the ancient Greek, English translation by John Brownlie (1857-1925) (*Crusader Hymns and Hymn Stories*, Billy Graham Evangelistic Association, 1967)
- "Jesus, Thou Joy of Loving Hearts" attributed to Bernard of Clairvaux, twelfth century (*Christian Hymns*, 2004)
- "Jerusalem the Golden" by Bernard of Cluny, twelfth century (*Christian Hymns*, 2004)
- "A Safe Stronghold Our God Is Still" and "Come Holy Spirit, God and Lord" by Martin Luther, sixteenth century (*Christian Hymns*, 2004)

- "O Sacred Head! Sore Wounded" and "Now Thank We All Our God" from the Lutheran tradition, seventeenth century (*Christian Hymns*, 2004)
- "O Come, All Ye Faithful" from the Latin, seventeenth century (*Christian Hymns*, 2004)
- "Praise to the Lord, the Almighty, the King of Creation" by Joachim Neander, seventeenth century (*Mission Praise*, 1983)
- "Let All the World in Every Corner Sing" by George Herbert, seventeenth century (*Mission Praise,* 1983)
- "Who Would True Valour See" and "Glory to Thee My God This Night' by John Bunyan and Thomas Ken, respectively; seventeenth century (*Christian Hymns*, 2004)
- "My Song Is Love Unknown" by Samuel Crossman, seventeenth century (*Christian Hymns*, 2004)

All but the last four of these hymns required translation before becoming part of the great wealth of English hymnody. In the sixteenth and seventeenth centuries, metrical versions of the Psalms existed in English, but it was in the eighteenth century that hymn writing began to flourish in England and other parts of the English-speaking world.

While some modern Christian songs are well worth singing, this book focuses on the great wealth of English hymnody inherited from past generations—in particular, the works of seven men and three women who number among the best and, in some cases, produced thousands of pieces. Isaac Watts (1674-1748) was the father of modern English hymnody. Charles Wesley (1707-1788) was the preeminent hymn writer of the evangelical revival that swept through Great Britain and its thirteen North American colonies in the 1730s and 1740s. Collaborating with William Cowper (1731-1800), the converted slave trader and Anglican evangelical John Newton (1725-1807) wrote *Olney Hymns*, which gained considerable popularity and yielded many print editions in both Great Britain and the United States. William Williams (1717-1791), called the sweet singer of Wales, was that country's chief hymn writer during the Methodist awakening. The other featured hymn writers lived in the nineteenth and early twentieth centuries and include Horatius Bonar (1808-1889), Philip Paul Bliss (1838-1876), Mrs. Cecil Frances Alexander (1818-1895), Frances Jane Crosby (1820-1915), and Eliza Edmunds Hewitt (1851-1920).

I hope my little book will, indeed, help readers to appreciate something of the great wealth of English hymnody which we have inherited from past generations. May these hymns continue to be sung in our churches, along with the best of the modern songs, and may my readers be so filled with the Holy Spirit and so joyful that they have a wonderful Savior that they cannot help singing, even when they are on their own!

ISAAC WATTS
(1674-1748)

Isaac Watts' *Hymns and Spiritual Songs* was first published in 1707. In addition to setting many of the Psalms to verse, he wrote about seven hundred hymns, earning him the reputation of the "Father of English Hymnody."

Actually, Watts' treatment of the Psalms exceeded simply putting them into verse. Not all of the early metrical psalms display the artistic merit of singular examples, like "All People that on Earth Do Dwell" from *The Whole Book of Psalms, Collected into English Meter* (published in 1562) or "The Lord's my Shepherd, I'll not Want" from *Scottish Psalter* (published in 1650). Also, since the Psalms were written many hundreds of years before the coming to earth of the Lord Jesus Christ, their metrical settings inherently lack the full Christian revelation.

Of course, the Psalms were, like the whole Bible, verbally inspired by the Holy Spirit. However, the Bible is a progressive revelation of truth and the Old Testament was a preparation for the coming of Christ in terms of the types and shadows and prophecies of the Old Covenant. Isaac Watts took the Psalms and Christianized them by making the latent patent and the prophetic historic. As a result, the Messianic Psalm 72 became "Jesus Shall Reign."

Jesus shall reign where'er the sun
Doth his successive journeys run;
His kingdom stretch from shore to shore,
Till moons shall wax and wane no more.

For Him shall endless prayer be made,
And praises throng to crown His head;
His name, like sweet perfume, shall rise
With every morning sacrifice.

People and realms of every tongue
Dwell on His love with sweetest song;
And infant voices shall proclaim
Their early blessings on His Name.

Blessings abound where'er He reigns:
The prisoner leaps to lose his chains;
The weary find eternal rest,
And all the sons of want are blest.

Where He displays His healing power,
Death and the curse are known no more;
In Him the tribes of Adam boast
More blessings than their father lost.

Let every creature rise and bring
Peculiar honours to our King;
Angels descend with songs again,
And earth repeat the loud Amen.[1]

Psalm 92 speaks of the blessings of the Sabbath in the original and of the blessings of the Lord's Day in Watts' version, "Sweet Is the Work, My God, My King." It is the day of rest and the day when we have time to think about God. Watts' version also goes on to speak about the eternal rest to which the Christian looks forward (Rev. 14:13).

Psalm 122 is one of the Songs of Ascents, written by King David for Israelites to sing as they went up to Jerusalem for the feasts of Passover, Pentecost, and Tabernacles. Watts' version, "How Pleased and Blest Was I," speaks of "David's greater Son" and describes Christians hearing "the sacred gospel's joyful sound" when they gather every Lord's Day.[2]

In Psalm 136:1-9, the psalmist details the wonders of creation. Then he recounts how the Lord Jehovah redeemed His people from Egypt by the blood of the Passover lamb and the power that divided the Red Sea (Psalm 136:10-15). Finally, verses sixteen through twenty-six give an account of God's leading through

---

[1] Isaac Watts, "Jesus Shall Reign Where'er the Sun," *Christian Hymns* (Bridgend: Evangelical Movement of Wales, 1985), 310.

[2] Isaac Watts, "How Pleased and Blest Was I," *Christian Hymns* (Bridgend: Evangelical Movement of Wales and Christian Hymns Committee, 2004), 368.

the wilderness to the land of Canaan. The psalmist uses type and shadow to speak of the wonders of redemption; in "Give to Our God Immortal Praise," Watts tells how God sent His Son with power to save and guides believers through this vain world to His heavenly seat. The psalm includes a chorus about God's mercy that appears at the end of each verse. Watts' rendering does the same, using *mercies* in the plural and three references to *wonders of grace*. I particularly like to sing such great themes to the serene and noble tune "Galilee."

Give to our God immortal praise;
Mercy and truth are all His ways:
Wonders of grace to God belong,
Repeat His mercies in your song.

Give to the Lord of lords renown,
The King of kings with glory crown;
His mercies ever shall endure,
When lords and kings are known no more.

He built the earth, He spread the sky,
And fixed the starry lights on high:
Wonders of grace to God belong,
Repeat His mercies in your song.

He fills the sun with morning light,
He bids the moon direct the night:

His mercies ever shall endure,
When suns and moons shall shine no more.

He sent His Son with power to save
From guilt and darkness and the grave:
Wonders of grace to God belong,
Repeat His mercies in your song.

Through this vain world He guides our feet,
And leads us to His heavenly seat:
His mercies ever shall endure,
When this vain world shall be no more.[3]

Psalm 146 is one of the great psalms of praise with which the book of Psalms ends. It begins, "Praise the LORD! Praise the LORD, O my soul! While I live I will praise the LORD; I will sing praises to my God while I have my being" (vv. 1-2). Watts' version, "I'll Praise my Maker While I've Breath," begins similarly but highlights the fact that Christians know that "our Savior Jesus Christ . . . has abolished death and brought life and immortality to light through the gospel" (2 Tim. 1:10). The vigorous tune "Monmouth" is a fitting setting.

I'll praise my Maker while I've breath,
And when my voice is lost in death,

---

[3] Isaac Watts, "Give to Our God Immortal Praise," *Psalms & Hymns of Reformed Worship* (London: The Wakeman Trust, 1991), 136.

Praise shall employ my nobler powers;
My days of praise shall ne'er be past,
While life, and thought, and being last,
Or immortality endures.[4]

Isaac Watts was a child prodigy. His father, also called Isaac, began the boy's education, including the study of Latin, when he was four years old. Mr. Watts was a godly man who took reading the Bible and prayer seriously, and young Isaac's affinity for poetry became evident in a time of family prayer.

"While they were at prayer, Isaac was heard to titter. His father demanded the cause of his merriment. 'Because,' he replied, pointing to the bell-rope by the fireplace, 'I saw a mouse run up that and the thought came into my mind: There was a mouse, for want of stairs, Ran up a rope to say his prayers.'"[5]

Less than two years later, the little boy wrote an acrostic poem, using the letters of his name, to prove his ability.

I am a vile polluted lump of earth,
So I've continu'd ever since my birth;
Although Jehovah grace does daily give me,
As sure this monster Satan will deceive me,

[4] Isaac Watts, "I'll Praise my Maker While I've Breath," *Christian Hymns* (Bridgend: Evangelical Movement of Wales and Christian Hymns Committee, 2004), 14.

[5] David G. Fountain, *Isaac Watts Remembered: 1674-1748* (Southampton: Mayflower Christian Bookshop), 12-13.

Come, therefore, Lord, from Satan's claws relieve me.

Wash me in Thy blood, O Christ,

And grace divine impart,

Then search and try the corners of my heart,

That I in all things may be fit to do

Service to Thee, and sing Thy praises too.[6]

His godly parents were greatly concerned that their son should be converted, and, no doubt, many prayers ascended to Heaven on his behalf. His personal papers bear witness to a definite concern for his soul's salvation in his early years, and young Isaac found "joy and peace in believing" (Rom. 15:13) at the age of fifteen.

The entirety of his life to this point was a time of historically fierce religious persecution. The Stuart kings showed no tolerance for Nonconformists, English Protestants who did not belong to the Church of England; and Mr. Watts was imprisoned more than once in consequence.

The Toleration Act of 1689 granted freedom of worship to Nonconformists, but they were still banned from pursuing a university education. Realizing that embracing these beliefs meant forfeiting his chance in academia, the brilliant young Isaac took his place among them, just as Moses chose "to suffer affliction with the people of God . . . esteeming the reproach of Christ greater riches than the treasures in Egypt" (Heb. 11:25-26).

---

[6] Fountain, 13-14.

When Isaac was sixteen, he attended a Nonconformist academy (the Nonconformist equivalent of a university) in London for four years. Upon completion of his education, he accepted a post in London as a tutor. Then, in 1699, he became the assistant pastor at Mark Lane Independent Church, accepting the position of senior pastor in 1702. The cause prospered, and the congregation moved to a new building, capable of seating 428, in 1709.

Three of Isaac's hymns speak about the cross. "Not All the Blood of Beasts on Jewish Altars Slain" draws upon types and shadows of the Old Testament sacrificial system. As the Israelites journeyed through the wilderness to Canaan, all the tribes pitched their tents surrounding the tabernacle, where they met with the Lord Jehovah.

The tabernacle itself had a single point of entry—a thirty-foot-wide screen of fine linen with blue, purple, and scarlet thread. This doorway symbolized the Lord Jesus Christ, the one and only Way to God. In John 14:6, Jesus says, "'I am the way, the truth, and the life. No one comes to the Father except through me.'"

The Israelites knew that "without shedding of blood there is no remission" (Heb. 9:22). When they passed through that gate, they brought an unblemished male bull or lamb (or, if they were poor, a turtledove or young pigeon) to be sacrificed. Placing their hand on the head of the offering demonstrated their trust in the offering as a substitutionary atonement for their sin. Then the animal was killed before the Lord.

At this point, the sons of Aaron sprinkled the blood around, skinned the animal, and cut it into pieces before burning the whole thing on the altar. The first chapter of Leviticus outlines the ritual in detail. This practice foreshadowed the one great Sacrifice of Calvary, which Isaac Watts understood and acknowledged when he wrote, "Not All the Blood of Beasts."

> Not all the blood of beasts,
> On Jewish altars slain,
> Could give the guilty conscience peace
> Or wash away the stain.

> But Christ, the heavenly Lamb,
> Takes all our sins away;
> A sacrifice of nobler name,
> And richer blood than they.

> My faith would lay her hand
> On that dear head of Thine,
> While like a penitent I stand,
> And there confess my sin.

> My soul looks back to see
> The burden Thou didst bear

When hanging on the cursed tree,
And knows her guilt was there.

Believing, we rejoice
To see the curse remove;
We bless the Lamb with cheerful voice,
And sing His wondrous love.[7]

Another great hymn about the cross, "Alas! and Did my Saviour Bleed," focuses on the greatness of the Person Who died there. John 1:29 says, "The next day John saw Jesus coming toward him, and said, 'Behold! The Lamb of God who takes away the sin of the world!'" The Person of our Savior gives infinite value to the sacrifice, making it sufficient for the whole world. "For God so loved the world that He gave His only begotten Son, that whoever believes in Him should not perish but have everlasting life" (John 3:16).

Although the blood of Jesus is sufficient to atone for the entire world's sin, the sinner must personally believe and trust in Jesus as his or her own Savior in order to have everlasting life. The hymn's final two verses portray the believer's proper response to such love, as described in Romans 12:1-2: "I beseech you therefore, brethren, by the mercies of God, that you present your bodies a living sacrifice, holy, acceptable to God, which is your reasonable service. And do not be conformed to this

---

[7] Isaac Watts, "Not All the Blood of Beasts," *Christian Hymns*, 589.

world, but be transformed by the renewing of your mind, that
you may prove what is that good and acceptable and perfect
will of God."

Alas! and did my Saviour bleed
And did my Sovereign die?
Would He devote that sacred head
For such a worm as I?

Was it for crimes that I had done,
He groaned upon the tree?
Amazing pity! Grace unknown!
And love beyond degree!

Well might the sun in darkness hide,
And shut his glories in,
When God, the mighty Maker, died
For man, the creature's sin.

Thus might I hide my blushing face
While His dear cross appears;
Dissolve my heart in thankfulness,
And melt my eyes to tears.

But drops of grief can ne'er repay
The debt of love I owe:

Here, Lord, I give myself away;
'Tis all that I can do.[8]

The well-known and highly regarded "When I Survey the Wondrous Cross" also illustrates the believer's response to the loving sacrifice of Jesus Christ.

When I survey the wondrous Cross
On which the Prince of glory died,
My richest gain I count but loss,
And pour contempt on all my pride.

Forbid it Lord that I should boast,
Save in the death of Christ my God:
All the vain things that charm me most,
I sacrifice them to His blood.

See from His head, His hands, His feet,
Sorrow and love flow mingling down:
Did e'er such love and sorrow meet
Or thorns compose so rich a crown?

Were the whole realm of nature mine,
That were an offering far too small,

---

[8] Watts, "Alas, and Did My Savior Bleed," *Christian Hymns*, 228.

Love so amazing, so divine,
Demands my soul, my life, my all.[9]

In "Come let Us Join Our Cheerful Songs," Watts reflects upon the scene portrayed in Revelation 5:8-14, as the cross is sung about in Heaven. He encourages Christians here on earth to join in cheerfully.

Come let us join our cheerful songs
With angels round the throne;
Ten thousand thousand are their tongues,
But all their joys are one.

"Worthy the Lamb that died," they cry,
"To be exalted thus!"
"Worthy the Lamb," our lips reply,
"For He was slain for us!"

Jesus is worthy to receive
Honour and power divine;
And blessings, more than we can give,
Be, Lord, for ever Thine.

---

9 Isaac Watts, "When I Survey the Wondrous Cross," *Psalms & Hymns of Reformed Worship* (London: The Wakeman Trust, 1991), 243.

Let all that dwell above the sky,

And air, and earth, and seas,

Conspire to lift Thy glories high,

And speak Thine endless praise.

The whole creation join in one,

To bless the sacred name

Of Him that sits upon the throne,

And to adore the Lamb.[10]

Another of Watts' hymns was evidently a favorite of William Carey, the great pioneer missionary. The final verse of "How Sad Our State by Nature Is" was written on his gravestone, when he was buried in Serampore, India.

How sad our state by nature is!

Our sin how deep it stains!

And Satan binds our captive minds

Fast in his slavish chains.

But there's a voice of sovereign grace

Sounds from the sacred Word—

Ho! ye despairing sinners, come,

And trust upon the Lord.

---

[10] Isaac Watts, "Come let Us Join Our Cheerful Songs," *Christian Hymns* (Bridgend: Evangelical Movement of Wales and Christian Hymns Committee, 2004), 142.

My soul obeys the almighty call,
And runs to this relief;
I would believe Thy promise, Lord;
O help my unbelief!

To the dear fountain of Thy blood,
Incarnate God, I fly;
Here let me wash my guilty soul
From crimes of deepest dye.

A guilty weak and helpless wretch,
On Thy kind arms I fall;
Be Thou my strength and righteousness,
My Jesus and my all.[11]

"Join All the Glorious Names" gives much glory and praise to the Lord Jesus Christ. The beautiful Welsh tune "Rhosymedre" is a lovely pairing with the words.

Join all the glorious names
Of wisdom, love, and power,
That ever mortal knew,
That angels ever bore;
All are too mean to speak His worth,
Too mean to set my Saviour forth.[12]

---

[11] Isaac Watts, "How Sad Our State by Nature Is," *Christian Hymns* (Bridgend: Evangelical Movement of Wales, 1985), 527.

Looking across Southampton Water from Western Shore toward the New Forest inspired Watts to write the opening verses of "There is a Land of Pure Delight." He then uses the analogy of the Israelites' crossing into their promised land of Canaan.

> There is a land of pure delight
> Where saints immortal reign;
> Infinite day excludes the night
> And pleasures banish pain.
>
> There everlasting spring abides,
> And never-withering flowers;
> Death, like a narrow sea, divides
> This heavenly land from ours.
>
> Sweet fields, beyond the swelling flood,
> Stand dressed in living green;
> So to the Jews old Canaan stood,
> While Jordan rolled between.
>
> But timorous mortals start and shrink
> To cross the narrow sea,
> And linger shivering on the brink,
> And fear to launch away.

[12] Isaac Watts, "Join All the Glorious Names," *Christian Hymns* (Bridgend: Evangelical Movement of Wales and Christian Hymns Committee, 2004), 165.

O could we make our doubts remove,
Those gloomy doubts that rise,
And see the Canaan that we love
With unbeclouded eyes;

Could we but climb where Moses stood,
And view the landscape o'er,
Not Jordan's stream, nor death's cold flood,
Should fright us from the shore.[13]

In the course of his life, Isaac Watts was recognized as the leader of the Nonconformists in London. In 1728, the universities of Edinburgh and Glasgow conferred upon him Doctorates of Divinity, and he became known as Dr. Watts.

God's providence shielded him from the persecution his father endured; Isaac's main suffering resulted from ill health that left him rather weak. A lifelong bachelor, he spent much of his life in the home of a Hertfordshire family, who took him in during a period of sickness in his late thirties.

His strength never returned after he suffered a stroke in 1739, and he died on December 11, 1748. His grave is located in Bunhill Fields among many heroes of the faith, including John Bunyan, Thomas Goodwin, and John Owen. Dear men! That is where their bodies are buried but their souls are in that "land of pure delight where saints immortal reign"!

---

[13] Watts, "There is a Land of Pure Delight," *Christian Hymns*, 863.

CHARLES WESLEY
(1707-1788)

For some people, not much time elapses between becoming compelled by the conviction of sin and need for salvation and making the decision to trust in the Lord Jesus Christ as Savior. However, this scenario was not the case for Charles Wesley nor his equally famous brother John.

The third surviving son of parish rector Samuel Wesley and his wife Susanna, Charles was born in the ancient town of Epworth in Lincolnshire, England, on December 29, 1707. His education started at home when he was five years old and continued there until he went to board at Westminster School in London at the age of eight. A 1733 graduate of Oxford University, he owned that Bible study and prayer became a pattern in his life only after the first two years of his university education, having previously been negligent of such things.

However, Charles became an ordained minister in the Church of England in 1735, the same year he set off with his brother John for the American colony of Georgia, where they hoped to minister to the Native Americans. The venture was a disaster; Charles returned to England just over a year later, and

John followed in January 1738. The chief problem was that they were not yet converted themselves. Rather than preaching the biblical doctrine of justification by faith, the Wesleys espoused a works-based dogma.

Three key testimonies influenced the brothers' spiritual journey upon their return to England. George Whitefield, a friend from Oxford days, was converted in 1735. By November 1737, he was preaching to large congregations in London twice each day.

Peter Böhler, one of the Moravian Christians with whom they were acquainted, taught at a religious society meeting in Fetter Lane, London. It was nominally associated with the Church of England. The Moravian Church dates back to the Bohemian Reformation, led by Jan Hus in the fifteenth century. Hus and fourteenth-century John Wycliffe are considered two great forerunners of the Protestant Reformation.

Charles' journal records that he first came across Martin Luther's commentary on Galatians on May 17, 1738. From it, he learned that the idea of justification by faith was not new in church history; actually, it was the great Reformer's chief teaching. Studying the commentary and Luther's *Preface* to Romans occupied several hours of his day. He meditated on Galatians 2:20, which says, "I have been crucified with Christ; it is no longer I who live, but Christ lives in me; and the life which I now live in the flesh I live by faith in the Son of God, who loved me and gave Himself for me."

His own conversion occurred just a few days later on May 21, which fittingly happened to be Whitsun (Pentecost Sunday) in the Church of England. Someone read to Charles from Psalm 32, which says, "Blessed is he whose transgression is forgiven, whose sin is covered. Blessed is the man to whom the LORD does not impute iniquity" (vv. 1-2). He later talked about how he tried to resist the truth of God's Word at the time, but the Holy Spirit persisted in gradually chasing away his unbelief. Eventually, he embraced faith in Christ.

Shortly thereafter, his brother John attended a meeting on Aldersgate Street and heard someone read from Luther's *Preface.* Having arrived in rather a depressed state of mind, he felt his heart lift as he listened and put his trust in Christ for salvation.

In the interim, Charles had written a hymn that the brothers and their friends sang together with great joy. Which particular song is unknown, but it could well have been "And Can It Be That I Should Gain," the first verse reflecting the personal emphasis Charles found in the words, "who loved *me* and gave Himself for *me*" (Gal. 2:20).

This hymn's sublime poetry is also scriptural—1 Peter 1:12, which speaks about "things which angels desire to look into," forms the basis for the second verse. "Emptied Himself," found in the hymn's third verse, draws upon the literal translation of Philippians 2:7a—"made Himself of no reputation." Jesus set aside the outward, visible manifestation of the Godhead without losing His Divine nature nor attributes.

The fourth verse ponders Charles' experience of conversion in light of Luke 4:18-19: "The Spirit of the Lord is upon Me, Because He has anointed Me to preach the gospel to the poor; He has sent Me to heal the brokenhearted, To proclaim liberty to the captives And recovery of sight to the blind, to set at liberty those who are oppressed; To proclaim the acceptable year of the Lord."

In the fifth verse, Charles celebrates his assurance of being justified by faith in the Lord Jesus Christ. "There is therefore now no condemnation to those who are in Christ Jesus" (Rom. 8:1a). The hymn sings well to the lively tune "Sagina."

> And can it be that I should gain
> An interest in the Saviour's blood?
> Died He for me, who caused His pain?
> For me, who Him to death pursued?
> Amazing love! How can it be
> That Thou, my God, shouldst die for me?
>
> 'Tis mystery all! The Immortal dies!
> Who can explore His strange design?
> In vain the first-born seraph tries
> To sound the depths of love divine!
> 'Tis mercy all! Let earth adore,
> Let angel minds inquire nor more.

He left His Father's throne above—
So free, so infinite His grace—
Emptied Himself of all but love,
And bled for Adam's helpless race:
'Tis mercy all! Immense and free;
For, O my God, it found out me!

Long my imprisoned spirit lay
Fast bound in sin and nature's night;
Thine eye diffused a quickening ray,
I woke, the dungeon flamed with light;
My chains fell off, my heart was free,
I rose, went forth, and followed Thee.

No condemnation now I dread;
Jesus, and all in Him is mine!
Alive in Him, my living Head,
And clothed in righteousness divine,
Bold, I approach the eternal throne,
And claim the crown, through Christ my own.[14]

In addition to Galatians 2:20, Psalm 32 played a part in Charles Wesley's conversion; and he wrote a metrical version about the blessing that is upon those who, as he expresses so

---

[14] Charles Wesley, "And Can It Be, That I Should Gain?" *Christian Hymns*, 509.

beautifully, "see the smiling face of heaven." It goes well with the beautiful tune "Lasis."

Blessed are they, supremely blest,
Whose wickedness is all forgiven,
Who find in Jesus' wounds their rest,
And see the smiling face of Heaven.

Blessed are they to whom the Lord
No more imputes iniquity,
Whose spirit is by grace restored,
And from all lies and guile set free.

But while, through pride, I held my tongue,
Nor owned my helpless unbelief,
My being languished all day long,
And conscience roared without relief.

Resolved, at last, to God I cried,
"I will my evil ways confess,
No more evade, or seek to hide
My depth of shameful sinfulness."

For this shall every child of God,
Thine all-surpassing love declare,

And take the grace on all bestowed,
Who pray the contrite sinner's prayer.

Blessed are they, supremely blest,
Whose wickedness is all forgiven,
Who find in Jesus' wounds their rest,
And see the smiling face of Heaven.[15]

Charles Wesley became a great hymn writer, penning more than sixty-five hundred hymns—many of high quality. W. Garrett Horder says:

> Amongst Charles Wesley's writings are to be found some of the grandest hymns in the English language. For spontaneity of feeling, his hymns are pre-eminent. They are songs that soar. They have the rush and fervour which bear the soul aloft . . . caught from the beating of his own heart, and the observation of hearts kindled by the great movement in which he bore so large a part.[16]

"O For a Thousand Tongues to Sing" was inspired by Peter Böhler, who mentioned that if he had a thousand tongues, he would use them all to praise the Redeemer. The seven-verse

---

[15] Wesley, "Blessed Are They, Supremely Blest," *Psalms & Hymns of Reformed Worship* (London: The Wakeman Trust, 1991), 32.

16 W. Garrett Horder, *The Hymn Lover: An Account of the Rise and Growth of English Hymnody* (London: J. Curwen and Sons, 1889).

hymn was originally part of a much longer poem, written on the first anniversary of Wesley's conversion. (Soon after this, he also, like Whitefield, began to regularly preach to crowds in public open spaces.) It is often sung to the tune "Lyngham" but is also effectively communicated by "Denfield."

O for a thousand tongues to sing
My great Redeemer's praise,
The glories of my God and King,
The triumphs of His grace.

My gracious Master and my God,
Assist me to proclaim,
To spread through all the earth abroad
The honours of Thy name.

Jesus! The name that charms our fears,
That bids our sorrows cease;
'Tis music in the sinner's ears,
'Tis life, and health, and peace.

He breaks the power of cancelled sin,
He sets the prisoner free;
His blood can make the foulest clean,
His blood availed for me.

He speaks, and, listening to His voice,
New life the dead receive,
The mournful broken hearts rejoice,
The humble poor believe.

Hear Him, ye deaf; His praise, ye dumb,
Your loosened tongues employ;
Ye blind, behold your Saviour come,
And leap, ye lame, for joy.

Look unto Him, ye nations, own
Your God, ye fallen race;
Look, and be saved through faith alone
Be justified by grace.[17]

"Jesus! The Name High Over All" similarly conveys Charles Wesley's desire to preach the gospel of Christ far and wide, which he accomplished as an itinerant minister for ten years, speaking to large groups of people.

Jesus! The Name high over all,
In hell, or earth, or sky;
Angels and men before it fall,
And devils fear and fly.

---

[17] Charles Wesley, "O for a Thousand Tongues," *Christian Hymns*, 556.

Jesus! The Name to sinners dear,
The name to sinners given;
It scatters all their guilty fear,
It turns their hell to heaven.

Jesus! The prisoner's fetters breaks,
And bruises Satan's head;
Power into strengthless souls it speaks,
And life into the dead.

O that the world might taste and see
The riches of His grace;
The arms of love that compass me
Would all mankind embrace.

His only righteousness I show,
His saving truth proclaim;
'Tis all my business here below
To cry, 'Behold the Lamb!'

Happy, if with my latest breath
I may but gasp His Name;
Preach Him to all, and cry in death,
'Behold, behold the Lamb!'[18]

---

[18] Charles Wesley, "Jesus! The Name High Over All," *Christian Hymns,* 171.

The fourth verse shows that his loving heart reflected, in a measure, that of his Master—he wanted everyone to be saved, as the Scriptures declare in Mark 16:15, John 3:16, 1 Timothy 2:3-4, and 2 Peter 3:9. This interpretation can be problematic for some people, in light of the doctrine of election. A discussion of this paradox appears in *Opening Up Romans* by the author of this book.[19]

This era was the time of the Great Awakening, an evangelical revival that swept through Great Britain and its thirteen North American colonies. The power of the Holy Spirit in the salvation of souls was much in evidence.

John the Baptist baptized people who responded to his preaching with water, but he predicted that Jesus would baptize "with the Holy Spirit and fire" (Luke 3:16). This promise was fulfilled at Pentecost and has been the experience of the Church in times of revival ever since. "O Thou Who Camest from Above," Charles Wesley's hymn about the Holy Spirit, provides good commentary on this truth. The tune "Wilton" conveys the fervor of the time in which the hymn was written.

> O Thou who camest from above
> The pure celestial fire to impart,
> Kindle a flame of sacred love
> On the mean altar of my heart!

---

[19] Peter Currie, "God's Plan and Purpose," *Opening Up Romans* (Leominster: Day One Publications, 2022).

There let it for Thy glory burn
With inextinguishable blaze,
And trembling to its source return
In humble prayer and fervent praise.

Jesus, confirm my heart's desire
To work and speak and think for Thee;
Still let me guard the holy fire,
And still stir up Thy gift in me.

Ready for all Thy perfect will,
My acts of faith and love repeat,
Till death Thine endless mercies seal,
And make the sacrifice complete.[20]

Every Christian *has* the Holy Spirit. Romans 8:9 says, "But you are not in the flesh but in the Spirit, if indeed the Spirit of God dwells in you. Now if anyone does not have the Spirit of Christ, he is not His." However, a Christian is not always *filled* with the Holy Spirit. The Book of Acts shows one baptism but many fillings. "And they were all filled with the Holy Spirit . . . And when they had prayed, the place where they were assembled together was shaken; and they were all filled with the Holy Spirit, and they spoke the word of God with boldness" (Acts 2:4; 4:31).

---

[20] Charles Wesley, "O Thou Who Camest from Above," *Christian Hymns*, 827.

Charles married Sarah Gwynne in 1749, and the couple made a home in Bristol. They traveled together until the responsibilities of raising their three surviving children and the effects of aging reduced their time on the road. By 1760, Charles gave up traveling altogether, and the family relocated to London in 1771. He wrote more hymns, many of which appeared in *A Collection of Hymns for the Use of the People Called Methodists,* published in 1780.

Late in March 1788, Sarah Wesley recorded the following words, composed by a severely weakened Charles. He died at the age of eighty-two on March 29 and is buried in Saint Marylebone's churchyard.

> In age and feebleness extreme,
> Who shall a sinful worm redeem?
> Jesus, my only hope Thou art,
> Strength of my failing flesh and heart;
> Oh, could I catch a smile from Thee,
> And drop into eternity![21]

Of Wesley's more than sixty-five hundred hymns, the following works stand out especially. They can be found in *Christian Hymns, 2004 Edition*:

- "Forth in Thy Name O Lord I Go" reflects the fact that worship is not only something done at church

---

[21] Arnold Dallimore, *A Heart Set Free: The Life of Charles Wesley* (Darlington: Evangelical Press, 1988), 250.

on Sunday but requires giving one's entire life to serving God.

- "Hark the Herald Angels Sing" is Wesley's great Christmas carol. Its equally great tune is an adaptation of Felix Mendelssohn's secular music, produced in 1855 by British musician William Hayman Cummings.

- "O Love Divine! What Have You Done," a quieter hymn, contemplates the Crucifixion, urging one to believe that it was for him or her and to realize that nothing else is worth thinking or speaking about in comparison. The end of every verse features the moving line, "My Lord, my Love is crucified."[22]

- "Jesu, Lover of my Soul" is one of the great hymns of the English-speaking church. It identifies the Lord Jesus Christ as the Refuge from the "storm of life"[23] and the One Who will "safe into the haven guide"[24] at the end of the journey. A number of other analogies are used as well, showing that the Lord Jesus is the all-sufficient Savior for every poor sinner.

- "Soldiers of Christ, Arise" reminds one that the Christian life is a battle against the world, the flesh,

---

[22] Charles Wesley, "O Love Divine! What Have You Done," *Christian Hymns* (Bridgend: Evangelical Movement of Wales and Christian Hymns Committee, 2004), 253.

[23] Wesley, "Jesu, Lover of my Soul" *Christian Hymns*, 550.

[24] Ibid.

and the devil. It teaches that salvation is like armor to protect and that "in the strength which God supplies,"[25] the victory can be won.

---

[25] Wesley, "Soldiers of Christ, Arise," *Christian Hymns,* 749.

JOHN NEWTON
(1725-1807)

John Newton's father, a seafaring man, owned a number of trading ships. His mother was a gentle Christian woman who taught her little boy the Scriptures and hoped that one day he would become a minister of the gospel. Sadly, she died when he was seven, at which time John was sent to boarding school. When he was only eleven years old, his father placed him on one of his ships, bound for Mediterranean posts.

Not surprisingly, John quickly picked up the ways and language of the seamen. When he returned home, he felt ashamed of his behavior but soon learned to dismiss the nagging of his conscience. Voyage followed voyage; and gradually, his conduct grew worse.

John's conscience did get to him when he was fifteen. He became quite religious for the next two years but then gave up his self-imposed discipline and went to the opposite extreme. Over the next five or six years, he endured harrowing experiences; he was treated badly and became a servant of slaves in Africa. He eventually ended up in Newfoundland. When he boarded the *Greyhound* on March 1, 1748, heading east for Great Britain, he was living in the gutter morally. His profanity shocked even his shipmates.

On March 9, the crew of the *Greyhound* found themselves in the midst of a tremendous storm. The ship, under attack from the violence of the sea, took on water faster than it could be pumped out yet somehow did not sink. John became startlingly aware of his own mortality as he pumped, understanding clearly that only the mercy of God could spare them. In the same moment, he realized he deserved no mercy and begged God for deliverance from the storm.

When he was off duty, John began to read the Bible in earnest, including the wonderful parable of the prodigal son in Luke 15. He said, "I felt that no one more perfectly fitted the picture of the prodigal than I did. The goodness of the father in not only receiving, but in running to meet such a son—an illustration of the Lord's goodness to returning sinners—deeply moved me."[26]

When John finally emerged from that harrowing voyage, he was a new man with a genuine love for the Lord Jesus and desire to follow Him. He continued a seafaring life for seven years before accepting an appointment as curate of Bedfordshire's Olney Parish Church in 1764. By this time, he was married to Mary Catlett, a fine Christian woman.

---

[26] Peter Masters, *Men of Destiny* (London: The Wakeman Trust, 2017), 93-94.

William Cowper met John in 1767 and soon became a fellow resident of the small Bedfordshire town. Out of this friendship grew an anthology of verses—268 by Newton and sixty-eight by Cowper—that were published as *Olney Hymns* in 1779, providing a source of hymns for the rural congregation who met under John's leadership during the week.

The most famous of these hymns, "Amazing Grace," is easily seen to be autobiographical in the early verses. I particularly like the six-verse version found in *Christian Hymns, 1985 Edition*, but omitting verse four. It could be observed that the first three verses get the singer all the way to glory, and the last two say what happens upon arrival.

> Amazing grace! how sweet the sound,
> That saved a wretch like me!
> I once was lost, but now am found;
> Was blind, but now I see.
>
> 'Twas grace that taught my heart to fear,
> And grace my fears relieved;
> How precious did that grace appear
> The hour I first believed!
>
> Through many dangers, toils and snares
> I have already come;
> 'Tis grace has brought me safe thus far,

And grace will lead me home.
Yes, when this flesh and heart shall fail,
And mortal life shall cease,
I shall possess within the veil
A life of joy and peace.

When I've been there a thousand years,
Bright shining as the sun,
I've no less days to sing God's praise
Than when I first begun.[27]

Having been converted on that harrowing voyage, John did indeed love the Lord Jesus very much, a devotion that is evident in one of his greatest hymns, "How Sweet the Name of Jesus Sounds." It has been set to two melodies, in particular, that serve it well—the modern "Rachel" and an older tune called "St. Peter."

How sweet the name of Jesus sounds
In a believer's ear!
It soothes his sorrows, heals his wounds,
And drives away his fear.

It makes the wounded spirit whole,
And calms the troubled breast;

---

[27] John Newton, "Amazing Grace," *Christian Hymns* (Bridgend, Evangelical Movement of Wales, 1985), 490.

'Tis manna to the hungry soul,
And to the weary, rest.
Dear name! the rock on which I build,
My shield and hiding-place,
My never-failing treasury filled
With boundless stores of grace.

Jesus! my Shepherd, Brother, Friend,
My Prophet, Priest and King,
My Lord, my Life, my Way, my End,
Accept the praise I bring.

Weak is the effort of my heart,
And cold my warmest thought;
But when I see Thee as Thou art,
I'll praise Thee as I ought.

Till then I would Thy love proclaim
With every fleeting breath;
And may the music of Thy name
Refresh my soul in death![28]

"Glorious Things of Thee Are Spoken" portrays "Zion, city of our God." Mount Zion was one of the mountains on which

---

[28] John Newton, "How Sweet the Name of Jesus Sounds," *Christian Hymns* (Bridgend: Evangelical Movement of Wales and Christian Hymns Committee, 2004), 152.

Jerusalem was built in Old Testament times, so Zion became a synonym for the city. The New Covenant replaces earthly types and shadows of the Old Testament with heavenly fulfilment, as described in Hebrews 12:22-24. The lyrics work well with Haydn's melody "Austria."

Glorious things of thee are spoken,
Zion, city of our God!
He whose word cannot be broken,
Formed thee for His own abode.
On the Rock of Ages founded,
What can shake thy sure repose?
With salvation's walls surrounded,
Thou may'st smile at all thy foes.

See! The streams of living waters,
Springing from eternal love,
Well supply thy sons and daughters,
And all fear of want remove:
Who can faint while such a river
Ever flows their thirst to assuage—
Grace, which, like the Lord the Giver,
Never fails from age to age.

Round each habitation hovering,
See! The cloud and fire appear,

For a glory and a covering,
Showing that the Lord is near:
Blest inhabitants of Zion,
Washed in the Redeemer's blood—
Jesus, whom their souls rely on,
Makes them kings and priests to God.

Saviour, if of Zion's city
I through grace a member am,
Let the world deride or pity,
I will glory in Thy name:
Fading is the worldling's pleasure,
All his boasted pomp and show;
Solid joys and lasting treasure
None but Zion's children know. [29]

"Let Us Love, and Sing, and Wonder" is a hymn in the strict meaning of that word, with a direct ascription of praise. Each verse speaks of the One Who has washed us with His blood. He is worthy of our noblest and most heartfelt praises.

Let us love, and sing, and wonder,
Let us praise the Saviour's Name!
He has hushed the law's loud thunder,

---

[29] Newton, "Glorious Things of Thee Are Spoken," *Christian Hymns*, 366.

He has quenched Mount Sinai's flame;
He has washed us with His blood,
He has brought us nigh to God.
Let us love the Lord who bought us,
Pitied us when enemies,
Called us by His grace and taught us,
Gave us ears, and gave us eyes:
He has washed us with His blood,
He presents our souls to God.

Let us sing, though fierce temptations
Threaten hard to bear us down!
For the Lord, our strong salvation,
Holds in view the conqueror's crown:
He who washed us with His blood,
Soon will bring us home to God.

Let us wonder; grace and justice
Join, and point to mercy's store;
When, through grace, in Christ our trust is,
Justice smiles, and asks no more.
He who washed us with His blood,
Has secured our way to God.
Let us praise, and join the chorus

Of the saints enthroned on high;
Here they trusted Him before us,
Now their praises fill the sky:
"You have washed us with Your blood;
You are worthy, Lamb of God."[30]

Newton's catalog of work also depicts a testimony of Christian living. "Begone, Unbelief; My Saviour Is Near" speaks somewhat autobiographically of the spiritual struggles he experienced as a believer.

"One There Is, Above All Others" reminds one that the Lord Jesus Christ is not only a wonderful Savior but also the best possible Friend that anyone could have, while "Quiet, Lord, My Froward [Perverse] Heart" expresses a simple, childlike faith, based on Psalm 131.

Each verse of "Though Troubles Assail, and Dangers Affright" ends with the Scriptural assurance that "the Lord will provide,"[31] a reference to Genesis 22:14, which says, "And Abraham called the name of the place, The-Lord-Will-Provide; as it is said to this day, 'In the Mount of the Lord it shall be provided.'" Fanny Crosby's grandmother would quote the first verse when Fanny's mother became sad because her child was blind.

---

[30] Newton, "Let Us Love, and Sing, and Wonder," *Christian* Hymns, 711.

[31] Newton, "Though Troubles Assail, and Dangers Affright," *Psalms & Hymns of Reformed Worship* (London: The Wakeman Trust, 1991), 511.

Though troubles assail,
And dangers affright,
Though friends should all fail,
And foes all unite—
Yet one thing secures us,
Whatever betide:
The Scripture assures us,
"The Lord will provide."[32]

In 1780, John Newton left Olney to become the minister of St. Mary Woolnoth in London, where he had an outstanding ministry for the remaining twenty-seven years of his life. He ordered the following words to be inscribed on his gravestone: "Once an infidel and libertine, a servant of slaves in Africa, was, by the rich mercy of our Lord and Saviour, Jesus Christ, preserved, restored, pardoned, and appointed to preach the faith he had long laboured to destroy."[33]

---

[32] Ibid.

[33] Masters, 97-98.

WILLIAM COWPER
(1731-1800)

Born in 1731, William Cowper (pronounced *Cooper*) was born into an Anglican home. His father was the rector of Great Berkhamsted in Hertfordshire. His kind, loving mother meant much to the little boy; she died when he was only six years old. Despite being a minister, the elder Mr. Cowper failed to share the gospel with his son, and William remained ignorant of the truth of the Scriptures at the boarding schools he attended, including Westminster School, where he was sent at the age of nine. His schooldays were marked by loneliness, insecurity, and bullying, though he also made some good friends at Westminster.

At the age of twenty-one, he was obliged to follow the legal profession, for which he had little interest, and began to suffer recurring bouts of severe depression. As the years passed, further setbacks took their toll: his father and stepmother died, and his closest friend drowned.

In 1763, he was offered the vacant post of clerk of the journals of the House of Lords. This position offered financial security, and he was required only to complete a straightforward public examination. But this prospect terrified William's despondent mind, and he attempted to take his own life.

A minister and Cambridge don, his brother John made every effort to help but to no avail. Rev. Martin Madan spoke to him about the wonderful truth of justification by faith in the Lord Jesus Christ; but at the time, it did not seem to offer comfort. Dr. Nathaniel Cotton, a physician and evangelical Christian, assumed responsibility for William's care in St. Albans.

William began to study the Bible and, a few months after entering the home, found the verse, "Whom God set forth as a propitiation by His blood, through faith, to demonstrate His righteousness, because in His forbearance God had passed over the sins that were previously committed" (Rom. 3:25).

The light of the gospel dawned on William. He recalled, "'Immediately I received strength to believe it and the full beams of the Sun of Righteousness shone upon me. I saw the sufficiency of the atonement He had made,[sic] my pardon was sealed in His blood . . . I could only look up to heaven in silent fear, overwhelmed with love and wonder.'"[34]

After eighteen months, he left Dr. Cotton's and moved to Huntingdon, near Cambridge. At first, this new situation proved to be challenging for him; he lived alone and could not cope with housekeeping.

---

[34] Elsie Houghton, *Christian Hymn-writers* (Bridgend: Evangelical Press of Wales, 1982), 149.

He became acquainted with a young man named William Unwin, and they found themselves of one mind in the gospel. An invitation to a meal with Unwin's parents followed, and William joined the household as a permanent lodger shortly thereafter.

The mother, Mary Unwin, was an excellent Christian lady. She helped care for William for most of the rest of his life. When the father died in 1767, Mary and their daughter, along with Mr. Cowper (as Mary Unwin always called him), moved about thirty miles away to Olney—the home of their friend John Newton.

The curacy of Olney kept Newton busy, and William helped him assist the poor and visit with the sick and dying. He always attended the mid-week meeting for prayer in the Great House. Newton said that William's prayers in public were offered with a humble heart but so earnestly that it was as if the Lord Jesus Christ were physically in the room and William spoke to Him face to face.

From time to time, William's mental health struggles returned; and partly as a diversion, Newton proposed that they start writing hymns. Over the next two years, William contributed sixty-eight hymns to their book, *Olney Hymns*.

"There Is a Fountain Filled with Blood" shows William's grasp of the gospel and remains popular among evangelical Christians to this day. The story is told of a preacher who did not hold fast to the great truths of the gospel. An elderly lady stood up and sang this hymn; and others soon joined her, making a worthy and effective response to the false message that was being preached. The tune "Evan" is a lively and suitable setting.

There is a fountain filled with blood
Drawn from Immanuel's veins;
And sinners plunged beneath that flood,
Lose all their guilty stains.

The dying thief rejoiced to see
That fountain in his day;
And there have I, though vile as he,
Washed all my sins away.

Dear dying Lamb, Thy precious blood
Shall never lose its power,
Till all the ransomed church of God
Be saved to sin no more.

E'er since by faith I saw the stream
Thy flowing wounds supply,
Redeeming love has been my theme,
And shall be till I die.

Then in a nobler, sweeter song
I'll sing Thy power to save,

When this poor lisping, stammering tongue
Lies silent in the grave.[35]

"Hark My Soul It Is the Lord" is unusual, though beautifully expressed, in that it puts scriptural words into the mouth of the Lord Jesus; it serves as a reminder of all He has done and will do for those who trust in Him and poses the question that was asked of Simon Peter after the resurrection in John 21:15-17.

Hark my soul! It is the Lord;
'Tis Thy Saviour, hear His word;
Jesus speaks, and speaks to Thee:
"Say, poor sinner lov'st thou Me?

"I delivered thee when bound,
And, when bleeding, healed thy wound;
Sought thee wandering, set thee right,
Turned thy darkness into light.

"Can a woman's tender care
Cease towards the child she bare?
Yes, she may forgetful be,
Yet will I remember thee.

---

[35] William Cowper, "There Is a Fountain Filled with Blood," *Christian Hymns* (Bridgend: Evangelical Movement of Wales and Christian Hymns Committee, 2004), 260.

"Mine is an unchanging love,
Higher than the heights above,
Deeper than the depths beneath,
Free and faithful, strong as death.

"Thou shalt see My glory soon,
When the work of grace is done;
Partner of My throne shalt be:
Say, poor sinner lov'st thou Me?"

Lord, it is my chief complaint
That my love is weak and faint;
Yet I love Thee, and adore;
O for grace to love Thee more![36]

Deep depression overtook William once again. For eleven months, he stayed at the Newtons' vicarage with Mrs. Unwin; and the friends helped him to the best of their ability. The final hymn he penned before relapsing was "God Moves in a Mysterious Way."

God moves in a mysterious way
His wonders to perform;
He plants His footsteps in the sea,
And rides upon the storm.

---

[36] Cowper, "Hark My Soul It Is the Lord," *Christian Hymns*, 698.

Deep in unfathomable mines
Of never failing skill
He treasures up His bright designs,
And works His sovereign will.

You fearful saints, fresh courage take;
The clouds you so much dread
Are big with mercy, and shall break
In blessings on your head.

Judge not the Lord by feeble sense,
But trust Him for His grace;
Behind a frowning providence
He hides a smiling face.

His purposes will ripen fast,
Unfolding every hour;
The bud may have a bitter taste,
But sweet will be the flower.

Blind unbelief is sure to err,
And scan His work in vain;
God is His own interpreter,
And He will make it plain.[37]

---

[37] Cowper, "God Moves in a Mysterious Way," *Christian Hymns*, 105.

Certainly, this theme was true to William's own experience. Why his early years had to be as they were is difficult, if not impossible, to explain; yet the Lord met him in Dr. Cotton's care home and saved him.

Eventually, the depression subsided, and Newton recorded that William was able to smile for the first time in more than a year but little or no spiritual recovery seemed to occur.

Mary Unwin also suffered a physical and mental breakdown. One of William's relatives moved them to Norfolk, but the era's oft-prescribed exposure to fresh air by the sea had little restorative effect. Even his conversion could not entirely eliminate his mental health challenges, although it gave him happy years of serving the Lord in Olney and the privilege of writing a number of immortal hymns that have blessed millions of Christians. Based on Matthew 6:25-34 and Habakkuk 3:17-18, "Sometimes a Light Surprises" is one such example.

Sometimes a light surprises
The Christian while he sings;
It is the Lord who rises
With healing in His wings:
When comforts are declining,
He grants the soul again
A season of clear shining,
To cheer it after rain.
In holy contemplation,

We sweetly then pursue
The theme of God's salvation,
And find it ever new.
Set free from present sorrow,
We cheerfully can say,
"Then let the unknown morrow
Bring with it what it may—

"It can bring with it nothing
But He will bear us through;
Who gives the lilies clothing
Will clothe His people too:
Beneath the spreading heavens
No creature but is fed;
And He who feed the ravens
Will give His children bread."

Though vine nor fig-tree neither
Their looked-for fruit should bear,
Though all the field should wither,
Nor flocks nor herds be there,
Yet God the same abiding,
His praise shall tune my voice;
For while in Him confiding,
I cannot but rejoice.[38]

---

[38] Cowper, "Sometimes a Light Surprises," *Christian Hymns,* 116.

It is sadly true that William did not end his days in this happy frame of mind; but he is happy now, singing the Lamb of God's power to save. Concerning the Heaven to where he has gone, the Scripture says, "And God will wipe away every tear from their eyes; there shall be no more death, nor sorrow, nor crying. There shall be no more pain, for the former things have passed away" (Rev. 21:4).

If any reader finds it impossible to understand why William Cowper suffered mentally as he did, a wise approach is to "trust in the Lord with all your heart, and lean not on your own understanding" (Prov. 3:5). A believer can find comfort by resting in the truth of the Scripture. "Above all, taking the shield of faith with which you will be able to quench all the fiery darts of the wicked one" (Eph. 6:16).

William Cowper died in April 1800. His earthly remains were laid to rest beside those of Mary Unwin, who predeceased him by four years. John Newton, age seventy-five, preached at his friend's funeral service, declaring, "What a glorious surprise must it be to find himself released from all his chains in a moment and in the presence of the Lord whom he loved and whom he served."[39]

---

[39] Houghton, 151.

WILLIAM WILLIAMS
(1717-1791)

It is generally agreed that was the sweet singer of Wales, just as King David was "the sweet psalmist of Israel" (2 Sam. 23:1). He wrote almost one thousand hymns in Welsh and over one hundred twenty in English, a few of which are translated from Welsh.

Mr. and Mrs. Williams, Nonconformists and Calvinists, welcomed the birth of their son William in 1717 at Cefn-coed Farm, near Llandovery, Carmarthenshire. William, himself, experienced conversion at the age of twenty after hearing Howell Harris, an early evangelist of the Calvinistic Methodist revival, preach in Talgarth churchyard. It proved to be the turning point in his life—a true Damascus Road experience.

The bishop of Saint David's oversaw William's ordination in 1740, after which he became a curate in Llanwrtyd and Llanddewi Abergwesyn in the northern part of Breconshire. The two parishes were small, but he felt called to travel from place to place and to preach wherever he could find people willing to listen to the gospel.

William resigned his curacy in 1744 and became assistant to Daniel Rowland, another of the early preachers of the evangelical revival in Wales. They were both members of the recently formed Calvinistic Methodist Association, which then existed within the established church. A few years later, William married Mary Francis; and they lived near Pantycelyn Farm, owned by his mother, not far from where he was born.

Daniel Rowland's powerful preaching influenced the conversions of thousands of people, but it was William Williams who set the Welsh singing the praises of the Lord. His poetic gift came to the attention of the Calvinistic Methodist Association at one of their early meetings; and from then on, he gave himself to writing hymns, as well as preaching the gospel, which he loved to do.

Two of his best hymns about the cross in English can be found in *Christian Hymns, 2004 Edition*. "Awake My Soul, and Rise" expresses awe over God's wonderful plan of salvation, which could not have been conceived by the human mind and amazes even angels. It is the message of "free salvation" that provides refuge and eternal security for every "wandering sheep" who trusts in Jesus because the redemption price was paid in full at the cross (Rom. 3:24).

Awake, my soul, and rise
Amazed, and yonder see

How hangs the mighty Saviour God
Upon a cursed Tree!

How gloriously fulfilled
Is that most ancient plan,
Conceived in the eternal mind
Before the world began.

Here depths of wisdom shine,
Which angels cannot trace;
The highest rank of cherubim
Still lost in wonder gaze.

Here free salvation reigns,
And carries all before;
And this shall for the guilty race
Be refuge evermore.

Now hell in all her strength,
Her rage, and boasted sway,
Can never snatch a wandering sheep
From Jesus' arms away.[40]

---

[40] Williams, "Awake My Soul, and Arise," *Christian Hymns,* 232.

"The Enormous Load of Human Guilt" focuses on the greatness of the price that our Savior paid, the love that motivated Him, and the rightness of singing His praises for all eternity. The depth of the tune "Lloyd" well fits such a great subject.

The enormous load of human guilt
Was on my Saviour laid;
With woes as with a garment He
For sinners was arrayed.

And in the fearful pangs of death
He wept; He prayed for me;
Loved and embraced my guilty soul
When nailed to the Tree.

O love amazing! Love beyond
The reach of human tongue;
Love which shall be the subject of
An everlasting song.

Eternity, though infinite,
Is short enough to trace
The virtues of His healing wounds,
The wonders of His grace.

Let men rejoice in Jesu's blood,
Let angels join our lays;
In one harmonious endless choir
Sing His eternal praise.[41]

"Jesus, Jesus All-sufficient" was originally written in Welsh and translated into English fairly recently by Robert Maynard Jones (1929-2017). Only two verses long, it is beautiful and fittingly set to the distinctively Welsh tune "Llwynbedw" in *Christian Hymns, 2004 Edition*. The hymn speaks of the Person of our Savior, which, after all, is what gives His sacrifice for us its infinite value.

Williams' most famous hymn, "Guide Me, O Thou Great Jehovah," is to the Welsh what "Abide with Me" is to the English. The first and last verses of "Abide with Me" are traditionally sung at the Football Association Challenge Cup Final, the oldest soccer competition in the world; "Guide Me, O Thou Great Jehovah" is often sung by the Welsh crowd at rugby matches.

It describes the Christian life, using Old Testament types and shadows—in particular, the journey through the wilderness to the Promised Land of Canaan. "Death of death and hell's destruction" refers to the description of the Day of Judgment in Revelation 20:11-15. This prospect is a fearful one to people who do not trust in Jesus as their Savior, but believers

---

[41] Williams, "The Enormous Load of Human Guilt," *Christian Hymns*, 259.

will land "safe on Canaan's side" when they cross from this life to the Heaven that awaits.

> Guide me, O Thou great Jehovah,
> Pilgrim through this barren land;
> I am weak, but Thou art mighty,
> Hold me with Thy powerful hand;
> Bread of heaven,
> Feed me till I want no more.
>
> Open Thou the crystal fountain
> Whence the healing stream doth flow;
> Let the fiery, cloudy pillar
> Lead me all my journey through;
> Strong Deliverer,
> Be Thou still my strength and shield.
>
> When I tread the verge of Jordan,
> Bid my anxious fears subside;
> Death of death and hell's destruction,
> Land me safe on Canaan's side;
> Songs of praises
> I will ever give to Thee.[42]

---

[42] Williams, "Guide Me O Thou Great Jehovah," *Christian Hymns,* 775.

William traveled extensively throughout Wales. Just days before his death, he wrote to Thomas Charles of Bala, observing ruefully that his treks of almost three thousand miles annually over half a century were reduced to the forty feet between his bed and fireside each day. He was content, however, in whatever the Lord had for him.

For decades, crowds of people came from all over Wales to hear Daniel Rowland preach in Llangeitho, where he ministered. When he heard songs of praise to the Lord descending the hillside, he would remark that the people had brought Heaven with them. They came to hear him preach the Word, but it was William Williams who set them singing.

Horatius Bonar
(1808-1889)

An entertaining anecdote once reached Horatius Bonar, mentioning a woman who had mistakenly assumed he was a long-dead medieval saint. While this impression was clearly false, Horatius *was* a saintly man of God who became the ordained minister of the North Parish Church in Kelso, Scotland, in 1837. In those days, Scotland experienced a great shower of blessing from on high, and Bonar's message—"'You must be born again'" (John 3:7)—rang repeatedly from his own church and in the Scottish Borders area of Scotland where his church was located.

The Church of Scotland suffered a serious split in 1843. Horatius numbered among many ministers who felt compelled to secede from the established church and join the newly formed Free Church of Scotland.

He ministered at Kelso for another twenty-three years, during which time he received an honorary Doctor of Divinity degree from the University of Aberdeen. Then, in 1866, the sixty members of the newly formed Chalmers Memorial Church in Edinburgh called Dr. Bonar as their minister.

By February 1867, the church had 170 members; and the membership continued to grow until, in July 1888, its number totaled 805. In addition to ministering to his growing congregation, Horatius preached in the open air and held children's meetings on the first Sunday evening of each month that attracted an attendance of up to sixteen hundred, even though the seating officially accommodated only a thousand!

He attended to all his daily duties with earnestness. His brother-in-law once said, "'One friend told him he was always writing, another that he was always preaching, a third that he was always praying—and a fourth might have added that he was always visiting.'"[43]

The author of over six hundred hymns and poems, Horatius is Scotland's premier hymn writer. He kept a notebook with him at all times to record any thought or inspiration that might prove useful. As a result, his hymns were written in any number of places—from railway carriages to firesides.

Two hymns of praise are suitable for commencing Lord's Day morning worship. "Rejoice and Be Glad! The Redeemer Has Come" recounts the entire story of Jesus, from the manger of Bethlehem to the return in glory. After every verse, the following chorus repeats.

---

[43] Graham L. Gibb, *Horatius Bonar and His Hymns* (Edinburgh: St. Catherine's Argyle Church, 1989), 12.

Sound His praises, tell the story of Him who was slain;
Sound His praises, tell with gladness He now lives again.[44]

The other hymn begins with a burst of Trinitarian praise, followed by words that reflect Revelation 1:5b-6, "To Him who loved us and washed us from our sins in His own blood, and has made us kings and priests to His God and Father, to Him be glory and dominion forever and ever. Amen."

Glory be to God the Father,
Glory be to God the Son,
Glory be to God the Spirit,
Great Jehovah, Three in One:
Glory, glory,
While eternal ages run!

Glory be to Him who loved us,
Washed us from each spot and stain;
Glory be to Him who bought us,
Made us kings with Him to reign:
Glory, glory,
To the Lamb that once was slain![45]

---

[44] Bonar, "Rejoice and Be Glad! The Redeemer Has Come," *Christian Hymns*, 287.

[45] Bonar, "Rejoice and Be Glad! The Redeemer Has Come," *Christian Hymns*, 44.

Perhaps his finest hymn, "I Heard the Voice of Jesus Say" could be named one of the greatest English hymns ever written; both autobiographical and Scriptural (Matt. 11:28; John 4:10; John 8:12), every Christian can joyfully sing it. The tune "Kingsfold" is a traditional English melody harmonized and arranged by Ralph Vaughan Williams (1872-1958) and is a wonderful melody for the words.

I heard the voice of Jesus say,
"Come unto Me and rest;
Lay down, thou weary one, lay down
Thy head upon My breast!"
I came to Jesus as I was,
Weary and worn and sad;
I found in Him a resting place,
And He has made me glad.

I heard the voice of Jesus say,
"Behold, I freely give
The living water; thirsty one,
Stoop down, and drink, and live!"
I came to Jesus, and I drank
Of that life-giving stream;
My thirst was quenched, my soul revived,
And now I live in Him.

I heard the voice of Jesus say,
"I am this dark world's Light;
Look unto Me, thy morn shall rise,
And all thy day be bright."
I looked to Jesus, and I found
In Him my Star, my Sun;
And in that light of life I'll walk,
Till travelling days are done.[46]

"Not What I Am, O Lord, but What Thou Art" is about the character of God. The Bible says that "God is light" (1 John 1:5), and "God is love" (1 John 4:8). He hates sin intensely but has a mighty heart of love for the sinner. It was when Moses learned something of this truth in Exodus 33:17 that he prayed, "Please, show me Your glory" (Exod. 33:18). The hymn's last verse echoes this request.

Not what I am, O Lord, but what Thou art!
That, that alone, can be my soul's true rest;
Thy love, not mine, bids fear and doubt depart,
And stills the tempest of my tossing breast.

Thy name is Love! I hear it from yon cross;
Thy name is Love! I read it in yon tomb;
All meaner love is perishable dross,
But this shall light me through time's thickest gloom.

---

[46] Bonar, "I Heard the Voice of Jesus Say," *Christian Hymns*, 579.

Girt with the love of God on every side,
Breathing that love as heaven's own healing air,
I work or wait, still following my guide,
Braving each foe, escaping every snare.

'Tis what I know of Thee, my Lord and God,
That fills my soul with peace, my lips with song;
Thou art my health, my joy, my staff and rod;
Leaning on Thee, in weakness I am strong.

More of Thyself, O show me hour by hour,
More of Thy glory, O my God and Lord;
More of Thyself, in all Thy grace and power;
More of Thy love and truth, incarnate Word![47]

"Peace"—or friendship with God—is one of the consequences of justification by faith in the Lord Jesus Christ. "Therefore, having been justified by faith, we have peace with God through our Lord Jesus Christ" (Rom. 5:1). Horatius mentions "this blood-sealed friendship" in the hymn "I Hear the Words of Love," emphasizing that it is unaffected by the vicissitudes of life.[48]

Christians do not lose salvation when they sin, but they do lose the joy of it. "If we say that we have no sin, we deceive

---

[47] Bonar, "Not What I Am, O Lord, but What Thou Art," *Christian Hymns*, 691.

[48] Bonar, "I Hear the Words of Love," *Christian Hymns*, 214.

ourselves, and the truth is not in us. If we confess our sins, He is faithful and just to forgive us our sins and to cleanse us from all unrighteousness" (1 John 1:8-9). A believer needs to confess sin to the Heavenly Father and obtain the daily cleansing that He offers in His Word. Thank God, the Christian always has a way back!

Bonar expresses this truth in "No, Not Despairingly."

No; not despairingly come I to Thee:
No; not distrustingly bend I the knee.
Sin hath gone over me,
Yet is this still my plea,
Jesus hath died.

Lord, I confess to Thee sadly my sin;
All I am tell I Thee, all I have been.
Purge Thou my sin away,
Wash Thou my soul this day,
Lord, make me clean.

Faithful and just art Thou, forgiving all;
Low at Thy pierced feet, Saviour I fall:
Oh, let the cleansing blood,
Blood of the Lamb of God,
Pass o'er my soul!

Then all is peace and light this soul within:
Thus shall I walk with Thee the Loved unseen,
Leaning on Thee, my God,
Guided along the road,
Nothing between.[49]

Like Isaac Watts' hymn "Not All the Blood of Beasts," Bonar's "No Blood, No Altar Now" extols how the cleansing power of Jesus' blood is superior over all the sacrifices of the Old Covenant.

In approaching God, either in private devotion or at church, one must own "truth in the inward parts" (Psalm 51:6), without any pretense, before confessing sin to the Heavenly Father. God's blessing is for people "in whose spirit there is no deceit" (Psalm 32:1-2). The first verse of "Help Me, my God, to Speak" shows that Horatius understood this concept well.

Help me, my God, to speak
True words to Thee each day;
Real let my voice be when I praise,
And trustful when I pray.[50]

---

[49] Bonar, "No, Not Despairingly," *Golden Bells* (London: Scripture Union, 1925), 214.

[50] Bonar, "Help Me, my God, to Speak," *Christian Hymns*, 394.

Moreover, worship is not something done only on the Lord's Day, nor even daily private devotions, important though these things are; it is giving one's entire life to serving God. "I beseech you therefore, brethren, by the mercies of God, that you present your bodies a living sacrifice, holy, acceptable to God, which is your reasonable service. And do not be conformed to this world, but be transformed by the renewing of your mind, that you may prove what is that good and acceptable and perfect will of God" (Rom. 12:1-2).

Horatius Bonar expresses this truth well in "Fill Thou My Life."

Fill Thou my life, O Lord my God,
In every part with praise,
That my whole being may proclaim
Thy being and Thy ways.

Not for the lips of praise alone,
Nor e'en the praising heart,
I ask, but for a life made up
Of praise in every part.

Praise in the common things of life;
Its goings out and in;
Praise in each duty and each deed,
However small and mean.

Fill every part of me with praise;
Let all my being speak
Of Thee and of Thy love, O Lord,
Poor though I be and weak.

So shalt Thou, Lord, from me, e'en me,
Receive the glory due;
And so shall I begin on earth
The song for ever new.

So shall no part of day or night
From sacredness be free;
But all my life, in every step,
Be fellowship with Thee.[51]

The Free Church of Scotland elected Dr. Bonar to be moderator of the General Assembly in 1883. Although a high honor, it was also a heavy responsibility for a man of seventy-five and led to a decline in his health. The last two years of his life were a time of weakness, suffering, and faith. He often repeated Psalm 103 from memory.

On July 31, 1889, his traveling days were over, and it was "heaven at last."[52] At his funeral, the congregation sang Bonar's own "Heaven at Last."

---

[51] Bonar, "Help Me, my God, to Speak," *Christian Hymns*, 816.
[52] Gibb, 15.

What a city, what a glory!
Far beyond the brightest story
Of the ages old and hoary;
Ah, 'tis heaven at last!

Christ Himself the living splendour,
Christ the sunlight mild and tender;
Praises to the Lamb we render;
Ah, 'tis heaven at last![53]

---

[53] Ibid.

Philip Paul Bliss
(1838-1876)

Philip Paul Bliss was born in northern Pennsylvania on July 9, 1838. He drew a picture of his childhood in the following poem.

Sweet little violets, born in the wild-wood;
Purest of loveliness, innocent childhood;
Shy as the antelope, brown as a berry,
Free as the mountain air, romping and merry.

Blue eyes and hazel eyes peep from the hedges,
Shaded by sun-bonnets frayed at the edges,
Up in the apple trees, heedless of danger,
Manhood in embryo stares at the stranger.

Out in the hilly patch, seeking the berries—
Under the orchard trees, feasting on cherries—
Trampling the clover blooms down 'mong the grasses,
No voice to hinder them, dear lads and lasses.

Dear little innocents! Born in the wild-wood;

Oh, that all little ones had such a childhood!

Heaven's blue over them, earth's green beneath them,

No sweeter heritage could we bequeath them.[54]

Philip first saw a piano around the age of ten. Walking through the village one day, he heard music floating through the open door of a nearby home. Rapt by the beautiful sound, Philip crossed the threshold and stood inside, silent and mesmerized—until the young lady stopped playing and he cried out to beg her for more. Less than charmed by the uninvited presence of this barefoot, gangly boy, she sent him away rather rudely. Philip obeyed, chagrined, but he carried with him the glorious memory.

He made his public profession of faith in Christ as a boy of eleven or twelve; in truth, however, he could never remember the time when he did not believe in Jesus as his Savior. His close friend, Major Daniel Whittle, attributed Philip's early conversion and consistent walk with God to the faithful prayers of his father.

He was twenty-two when Normal Academy of Music, a traveling school for aspiring music teachers, came to New York for six weeks in 1860. Philip had attended a local singing school and acquired enough education to enable him to teach, and this

---

[54] Philip Bliss, *Memoirs of Philip P. Bliss,* D.W. Whittle, ed. (New York: A.S. Barnes and Company, 1877), 156.

opportunity was just what he needed. But the fee was thirty dollars, which was way beyond what he could afford.

His wife's grandmother saw him, disappointed and in tears over the impossibility of the situation. Upon hearing the cause of his distress, she offered to contribute the whole of her savings—various and sundry pieces of silver she had dropped into a stocking over the course of many years. If it were enough, he was welcome to it.

It was enough, and he accepted the money gratefully. By the end of that year, he was ready to start as a professional music teacher.

In 1864, the Blisses moved to Chicago. The next year, Philip was offered a position at Root and Cady Musical Publishers. During this time, he began to compose, producing popular sentimental pieces at first before transitioning to songs that convey the truths of the gospel.

In July 1870, Philip became leader of the choir of the First Congregational Church of Chicago; and a few months later, the superintendent of the Sunday school, serving hundreds of children. These occupations continued until March 25, 1874, when he began his career as a singing evangelist in collaboration with Major Whittle, who did most of the preaching. Over the next three years, their combined ministry was greatly blessed, witnessing the salvation of hundreds of souls.

Philip wrote "Hold the Fort" after hearing Major Whittle, a Union Army veteran, talk about the Battle of Allatoona Pass.

Moving northward after the fall of Atlanta, the Confederates planned to take the pass and destroy not only the railroad, which was General Sherman's line of communication, but also a vital supply depot.

After surrounding the camps, the Confederates sent a note to the enemy's command, offering to minimize bloodshed by accepting their surrender. Sherman's reinforcements were on the march, though, and his message to Allatoona via signal flag preceded them: "Hold the Fort; I am coming. W. T. Sherman."

The Union general refused to concede, and sharp fighting commenced. The Confederates drove the Union defenses inward to "a small fort upon the crest of the hill." Casualties were high, and it seemed pointless to fight on, but this was the moment when Sherman's signal flag message was seen. "Cheers went up . . . and . . . they held the fort for three hours, until the advance guard of Sherman's army came up." The Confederates had no choice but to withdraw.[55]

This battle can be used to describe the motivation Christians can draw both from the gracious help that the Lord Jesus Christ supplies in the battles of life and also from the ultimate hope of His glorious appearing. "But hold fast what you have till I come . . . Behold, I am coming quickly! Hold fast what you have, that no one may take your crown" (Rev. 2:25; 3:11). Whittle recalled that Philip immediately had the idea for the hymn and published the sheet music right away.

---

[55] Bliss, *Memoirs of Philip P. Bliss*, 68-70.

Ho, my comrades! See the signal
Waving in the sky!
Reinforcements now appearing,
Victory is nigh!

(chorus)
"Hold the fort, for I am coming!"
Jesus signals still;
Wave the answer back to heaven,
"By Thy grace we will!"

See the mighty host advancing,
Satan leading on:
Mighty men around us falling,
Courage almost gone!
(chorus)

See the glorious banner waving!
Hear the trumpet blow!
In our Leader's name we'll triumph
Over every foe!
(chorus)

Fierce and long the battle rages,
But our help is near:

> Onward comes our great Commander,
>
> Cheer, my comrades, cheer!
>
> *(chorus)*[56]

Philip wrote his own tunes, as well as the melodies for other great hymns, such as Horatio Gates Spafford's "When Peace, Like a River" and Arthur T. Pierson's "With Harps and with Vials [Bowls]."

Perhaps Philip's greatest hymn is "Man of Sorrows! What a Name," borrowing the description of the Lord Jesus Christ found in Isaiah 53:3. Focusing on the cross, each verse explains something of what was accomplished there before rising to a crescendo with the words, "Hallelujah! What a Saviour!" The final verse is a fitting climax, speaking of His Second Coming as our glorious King and saying that the hallelujahs will be renewed in Heaven.

> Man of Sorrows! What a name
>
> For the Son of God, who came
>
> Ruined sinners to reclaim!
>
> Hallelujah! What a Saviour!

> Bearing shame and scoffing rude,
>
> In my place condemned He stood;

---

[56] Bliss, "Hold the Fort," *Sacred Songs & Solos* (London: Marshall, Morgan & Scott, 1977), 669.

Sealed my pardon with His blood:
Hallelujah! What a Saviour!

Guilty, vile, and helpless, we;
Spotless Lamb of God was He:
Full atonement! Can it be?
Hallelujah! What a Saviour!

Lifted up was He to die,
"It is finished!" was His cry;
Now in heaven exalted high:
Hallelujah! What a Saviour!

When He comes our glorious King,
All His ransomed home to bring,
Then anew this song we'll sing:
Hallelujah! What a Saviour! [57]

"Once for All," another of Philip's hymns begins, "Free from the law, oh, happy condition!" While the Ten Commandments are "holy and just and good" (Rom. 7:12), they are not the way of salvation. "Therefore by the deeds of the law no flesh will be justified in His sight, for by the law is the knowledge of sin" (Rom. 3:20). Ephesians 2:8-9 states clearly, "For by grace you have been saved through faith, and that not of yourselves;

---

[57] Bliss, "Man of Sorrows! What a Name," *Christian Hymns,* 248.

it is the gift of God, not of works, lest anyone should boast." Grace is the free, unmerited favor of God, and faith must be placed simply and solely in the Lord Jesus Christ and what He accomplished for us at Calvary's cross. Some people are not bold enough to believe that it can be that simple, but it is (Matt. 11:28; Luke 7:48-50; John 3:14-16; Acts 13:38-39, 15:10-11; Rom. 1:16-17; Gal. 3:13-14)!

Free from the law, oh, happy condition!
Jesus hath bled, and there is remission!
Cursed by the law, and bruised by the Fall,
Grace hath redeemed us once for all.

(chorus)
Once for all, O sinner receive it;
Once for all, O brother believe it:
Cling to the Cross, the burden will fall;
Christ hath redeemed us once for all.

Now we are free—there's no condemnation,
Jesus provides a perfect salvation;
"Come unto Me"—oh, hear His sweet call!
Come, and He saves us once for all.
(chorus)

"Children of God!" oh, glorious calling!
Surely His grace will keep us from falling;
Passing from death to life at His call,
Blessed salvation once for all.
(chorus)[58]

Much of Philip's work focused on the glorious gospel. "One Offer of Salvation" is a lovely gospel song about the only hope for poor sinners—"Christ, the Cornerstone . . . Christ, the Living Way...the Cross of Calvary."[59]

"Whosoever Will" echoes the message of Revelation 22:17 and exults in the fact that the gospel is now going out into all the world and that anyone may accept the Savior's free gift of salvation and eternal life. "Almost Persuaded Now to Believe" speaks lovingly and earnestly to people who feel drawn to the Lord Jesus Christ but are tempted to delay coming to Him for salvation.

"Let the Lower Lights Be Burning" likens the mercy of God to a lighthouse, shining for vessels in peril on the sea; the hymn also stresses that the lower lights, which represent the lives of humble Christian people, also need to be burning. Matthew 5:14-16 says, "You are the light of the world. A city that is set on a hill cannot be hidden. Nor do they light a lamp and put it under a basket, but on a lampstand, and it gives light to all who

---

[58] Bliss, "Once for All," *Sacred Songs & Solos*, 143.

[59] Bliss, "One Offer of Salvation," *Sacred Songs & Solos*, 84.

are in the house. Let your light so shine before men, that they may see your good works and glorify your Father in heaven."

Some of Philip's songs apply particularly to children and young people, as well as adults. The chorus of one such example begins, "I am so glad that Jesus loves me."[60] It is a reminder that the greater thing is not that we love Jesus but that He loves us. "In this is love, not that we loved God, but that He loved us and sent His Son to be the propitiation for our sins" (1 John 4:10).

"Dare to Be a Daniel" is also particularly suitable for young people, though its leading thought is important for all ages. This chorus follows the end of each verse.

Dare to be a Daniel!
Dare to stand alone!
Dare to have a purpose firm!
Dare to make it known.[61]

Through Jade Gate and Central Asia, by pioneer missionaries Mildred Cable and Francesca French, gives an account of their journeys with Evangeline French in Northwest China and Central Asia during the 1920s. Their outreach included a special children's service that clearly left an impression.

---

[60] Bliss, "I Am So Glad That Our Father in Heav'n," *Golden Bells* (London: Scripture Union, 1925), 685.

[61] Bliss, "Dare to Be a Daniel," *Golden Bells* 510.

One little fellow, unconscious that he was being watched, walked down the street singing at the top of his voice, "Dare to be a Daniel, dare to stand alone" [presumably in Chinese]; then coming to a stop before a peanut vendor, and looking him in the face, said, "Did you *know* that there is only *One* God? and *One* Lord Jesus Christ?" "Why, no," said the old man, bewildered. "Well, it is true," answered the child, and passed on singing, "Dare to have a purpose true, and dare to make it known."[62]

The beautiful "Wonderful Words of Life" reiterates the Gospel of John, which is full of such sayings (John 3:16; 4:10; 5:24; 6:63; 20:30-31); the tune Philip Bliss wrote fits it perfectly.

> Sing them over again to me,
> Wonderful words of life!
> Let me more of their beauty see,
> Wonderful words of life!
> Words of life and beauty,
> Teach me faith and duty!

(chorus)

Beautiful words! Wonderful words! Wonderful words of life!
Beautiful words! Wonderful words! Wonderful words of life!

---

[62] Mildred Cable and Francesca French *Through Jade Gate and Central Asia* (London: Hodder and Stoughton, 1943), 123-24.

Christ, the blessed One, gives to all
Wonderful words of life!
Sinner, list to the loving call,
Wonderful words of life!
All so freely given,
Wooing us to heaven!
(chorus)

Sweetly echo the gospel call!
Wonderful words of life!
Offer pardon and peace to all!
Wonderful words of life!
Jesus, only Saviour,
Sanctify for ever!
(chorus)[63]

The word *more* is a good motto for the Christian. In his first epistle to the Thessalonians, the apostle Paul commends their "faith and love" (1 Thess. 3:6) but goes on to say that he was praying for an opportunity to "perfect what is lacking in your faith" (1 Thess. 3:10) and that the Lord would "make you increase and abound in love" (1 Thess. 3:12). Believers should never rest on their laurels but always focus on moving forward, as Paul admonishes in Philippians 3:12-14.

---

[63] Bliss, "Wonderful Words of Life," *Sacred Songs & Solos*, 357.

Philip expressed this idea in "More Holiness Give Me," which he called "My Prayer."

More holiness give me,
More strivings within;
More patience in suffering,
More sorrow for sin;
More faith in my Saviour,
More sense of His care;
More joy in His service,
More purpose in prayer.

More gratitude give me,
More trust in the Lord;
More zeal for His glory,
More hope in His Word;
More tears for His sorrows,
More pain at His grief;
More meekness in trial,
More praise for relief.

More purity give me,
More strength to o'ercome;
More freedom from earth-stains,
More longings for home.
More fit for the kingdom,

> More used would I be;
> More blessed and holy,
> More, Saviour, Like Thee.[64]

Tragedy struck at the end of 1876, bringing an abrupt end to Philip Bliss's work on earth. He and his wife, along with their two sons, had just spent a happy Christmas with her parents and her grandmother, who had so generously funded Philip's tuition in the singing school. On December 28, he took his two little boys aside and prayed with them, bade goodbye to all, and, standing upon the threshold for a moment, said, "I would love to stay. I would far rather stay than go, if it were God's will; but I must be about the Master's work."[65]

Philip and his wife embarked on the long train journey to Chicago, but they never arrived. A bridge collapsed near Ashtabula, Ohio, plunging the train into an icy river bed. In spite of the wintry conditions, the train caught fire, and the majority of the passengers were burned to death, including Philip and Lucy Bliss.

One of the last hymns he wrote is the enduringly popular "I Will Sing of My Redeemer." His lifelong friend, James McGranahan, wrote the original music after Philip's death. (McGranahan wrote both words and music of the excellent hymn "O What a Saviour that He Died for Me.") He also stepped

---

[64] Bliss, "More Holiness Give Me," *Sacred Songs and Solos*, 582.

[65] Bliss, *Memoirs of Philip P. Bliss*, 93.

into Philip's place in the evangelistic work with Major Whittle. My mother loved this particular hymn and told me on one occasion that she had been singing it repeatedly.

I will sing of my Redeemer,
And His wondrous love to me;
On the cruel Cross He suffered,
From the curse to set me free.

(chorus)
Sing, O sing of my Redeemer!
With His blood He purchased me,
On the cross He sealed my pardon,
Paid the debt and made me free.

I will tell the wondrous story,
How my lost estate to save,
In His boundless love and mercy,
He the ransom freely gave.
(chorus)

I will praise my dear Redeemer,
His triumphant power I'll tell,
How the victory He giveth
Over sin and death and hell.
(chorus)

I will sing of my Redeemer,

And His heavenly love to me;

He from death to life hath brought me,

Son of God with Him to be.

(chorus)[66]

Where are Philip and Lucy Bliss now? Their mortal remains were burned to ashes by that terrible fire, but is that all? Of course not! An inner man, an inner woman, survives death—what the Bible calls the soul. Where are their souls? Philip's hymn "Hallelujah! 'Tis Done!" gives the answer.

'Tis the promise of God full salvation to give

Unto him who on Jesus His Son will believe.

(chorus)

Hallelujah! 'Tis done; I believe on the Son;

I am saved by the blood of the Crucified One!

Hallelujah! 'Tis done; I believe on the Son;

I am saved by the blood of the Crucified One!

Though the pathway be lonely and dangerous too,

Surely Jesus is able to carry me through.

(chorus)

---

[66] Bliss, "I Will Sing of My Redeemer," *Christian Hymns*, 155.

Many loved ones have I in yon heavenly throng—
They are safe now in glory and this is their song:
(chorus)

Little children I see standing close by their King,
And He smiles, as their song of salvation they sing:
(chorus)

There are prophets and kings in that throng I behold,
And they sing as they march through the streets of pure gold:
(chorus)

There's a part in that chorus for you and for me,
And the theme of our praises for ever will be:
(chorus)[67]

The third verse of this glorious hymn speaks about the "many loved ones" who are no longer on earth. Bliss is looking by faith across the narrow sea of death, and he can see the countless heavenly throng in the land of pure delight where saints immortal reign. It is made up of all who believe on the Son as their Savior; he says "they are safe now in glory." [68] That is the point! The bodies of Philip and Lucy Bliss perished in the flames at Ashtabula, but their immortal souls went straight to be

---

[67] Bliss, "Hallelujah! 'Tis Done!," *Sacred Songs & Solos*, 841.
[68] Ibid.

with the Lord Jesus Christ, and that is where they are now—safe in glory!

After Philip and Lucy died, an eight-year-old German boy named William Herschberger wrote to Major Whittle to say that he realized his need of a Savior while singing Philip's hymn "Hallelujah, 'Tis Done" during a meeting. When Major Whittle extended an invitation to unbelievers who wished to make a decision for the Lord, William rose to request prayer. He did well to stop and think whether the words of the hymn were really true of himself.

There is a Heaven to gain and a Hell to shun. In Acts 16:30, the apostle Paul was asked, "What must I do to be saved?" The answer rang out clear and plain: "'Believe on the Lord Jesus Christ and you will be saved'" (Acts 16:31).

Believe on Jesus as your Savior, put your trust in Him, and then, when your time comes, your immortal soul will likewise go straight to glory to join in the everlasting song of praise to Him. Amen!

The great evangelist D.L. Moody described Philip as being not only greatly honored by God but also most humble. He believed that God equipped Philip Bliss to write hymns for the Church in that time, just as He had Charles Wesley in his own. He praised God for the many hundreds of souls the world over who were brought to a saving knowledge of Christ as a result of Philip's hymns.

FRANCES JANE CROSBY
(1820-1915)

The previous seven hymn writers featured have all been men. The early days of English hymnody do seem to present a paucity of women. However, this imbalance is about to be rectified.

On March 24, 1820, a little girl was born in the state of New York. Six weeks later, a treatment for an eye infection left her permanently blind. The little girl's name was Frances Jane Crosby.

Although she was blind, Fanny Crosby climbed trees, played games with other children, and rode bareback on her grandpa's old horse, Dobbin. Her grandmother was a lovely Christian lady who significantly influenced Fanny's upbringing. She told Fanny about the kind Heavenly Father Who sent His only Son, Jesus Christ, into the world to be Savior and Friend.

When Fanny was eight or nine years old, people kept saying she could not do this or that because she was blind. Upset, she decided to speak to God, the kind Heavenly Father; and she suddenly knew God was telling her not to be sad—Fanny was going to be happy and useful in her blindness. She wrote a poem to express how she felt.

> Oh what a happy soul I am!
> Although I cannot see,
> I am resolved that in this world
> Contented I will be.

> How many blessings I enjoy
> That other people don't!
> To weep and sigh because I'm blind
> I cannot and I won't.[69]

Fanny was fifteen when a fine new school for the blind opened in New York City. She was able to learn everything that the best schools for sighted students taught. She was happy, though one subject she did not like.

> I loathe, abhor, it makes me sick
> To hear the word arithmetic![70]

Apart from that, she progressed well and enjoyed English, history, philosophy, and science. She later became one of the teachers at the school and married a colleague, Alexander Van Alstyne, just before her thirty-eighth birthday.

---

[69] Fanny J. Crosby, *Memories of Eighty Years* (London: Hodder and Stoughton, 1908), 16.

[70] Lucille Travis, *The Blind Girl's Song* (Fearn: Christian Focus, 2013), 38.

The death of their only child in early infancy was a deep sorrow. Fanny's lifelong friend Anna reminded her of a poem she had written for her own mother when her infant sister died, recalling her firm belief that the child was with Jesus. Anna encouraged Fanny to find comfort in the knowledge that her sister and daughter were together with the Lord, and, eventually, she did.

Before her marriage, Fanny collaborated with George Root to write secular songs but it was not until about six years after she married that she started writing hymns and gospel songs, a practice she continued for the remaining fifty years of her life. In all, she penned more than eight thousand hymns and stands alongside the great hymn writers in the history of English hymnody. Although, strictly speaking, she was Mrs. Van Alstyne, she continued to be known to the wider public as Fanny Crosby.

Fanny was, without doubt, a born-again believer. In her younger years, she grew somewhat indifferent to Christian things; but when she was thirty years old, she dreamed that a good friend asked her if they would meet in Heaven. It made her stop and think, as her grandmother had asked her the same thing on her deathbed many years earlier.

Soon after the dream, in the autumn of 1850, the Thirtieth Street Methodist Church in New York City held evangelistic meetings. Fanny attended with friends every evening, searching for spiritual joy. On November 20, she went forward to pray. As the congregation sang "Here, Lord, I give myself away" from Isaac Watts' hymn "Alas! and Did My Savior Bleed," a heavenly light filled her soul; and she jumped up, shouting praise to the Lord.

It is possible to discern a lot about Fanny's spiritual life from her hymns. "Pass Me Not" shows her clear grasp of the way of salvation. The first verse gives the seeking soul a voice. The second shows the need for the "godly sorrow [that] produces repentance" (2 Cor. 7:10), the third, the need for a trusting faith in the free, unmerited favor of God described in Ephesians 2:8-9. The fourth relays how much the Lord Jesus means to those who do trust in Him as their Savior.

Pass me not, O gentle Saviour,

Hear my humble cry;

While on others Thou art calling,

Do not pass me by.

(chorus)

Saviour! Saviour!

Hear my humble cry

And while others Thou art calling,

Do not pass me by.

Let me at a throne of mercy

Find a sweet relief;

Kneeling there in deep contrition,

Help my unbelief.

(chorus)

Trusting only in Thy merit,

Would I seek Thy face;

Heal my wounded broken spirit,

Save me by Thy grace.

(chorus)

Thou the spring of all my comfort,

More than life to me,

Whom have I on earth beside Thee?

Whom in heaven but Thee?

(chorus)[71]

Fanny's entire life was consecrated to the service of God, and she loved to spend time before the throne of grace in prayer. She knew that perfection is never achieved in this life and that people always need to pray the Lord draws them ever nearer to Himself, as she reflects in "I Am Thine, O Lord."

I am Thine, O Lord; I have heard Thy voice,

As it told Thy love to me,

---

[71] Fanny Crosby, "Pass Me Not," *Christian Hymns,* 561.

But I long to rise in the arms of faith
And be closer drawn to Thee.

(chorus)
Draw me nearer, nearer, blessed Lord,
To the Cross where Thou hast died;
Draw me nearer, nearer, nearer, blessed Lord,
To Thy precious wounded side.

Consecrate me now to Thy service, Lord,
By the power of grace divine;
Let my soul look up with a steadfast hope
And my will be lost in Thine.
(chorus)

Oh, the pure delight of a single hour
That before Thy throne I spend,
When I kneel in prayer and with Thee, my God,
I commune as friend with Friend.
(chorus)

There are depths of love that I cannot know,
Till I cross the narrow sea;
There are heights of joy that I may not reach,
Till I rest in peace with Thee.
(chorus)[72]

---

[72] Crosby, "I Am Thine, O Lord," *Golden Bells,* 483.

Fanny was quite burdened about the salvation of souls. She spoke in prisons and supported the work of mission churches in some of New York City's most impoverished areas. She lived simply in a rundown apartment and was a bright witness to her neighbors, some of whom loved her very much. "Rescue the Perishing" conveys her concern for them all.

Rescue the perishing, care for the dying,
Snatch them in pity from sin and the grave;
Weep o'er the erring one, lift up the fallen,
Tell them of Jesus, the Mighty to save.

(chorus)
Rescue the perishing, care for the dying;
Jesus is merciful, Jesus will save.

Though they are slighting Him, still He is waiting,
Waiting the penitent child to receive:
Plead with them earnestly, plead with them gently;
He will forgive if they only believe.
(chorus)

Down in the human heart, crushed by the tempter,
Feeling lie buried that grace can restore;
Touched by a loving hand, wakened by kindness,
Chords that were broken will vibrate once more.

(chorus)

> Rescue the perishing, duty demands it;
> Strength for Thy labour the Lord will provide:
> Back to the narrow way patiently win them;
> Tell the poor wanderer a Saviour has died.
> *(chorus)*[73]

Howard Doane composed melodies for many of Fanny's hymns. "[His] music was easy to remember when people heard it once or twice. The people Fanny hoped to reach with her songs didn't have pianos, were too poor to own hymnals, and the songs they heard in church really needed to be the kind they could easily memorize."[74]

"A Few More Marchings Weary" reflects that the Christian life is not easy, but the hope of Heaven enables believers to press on cheerfully. "Jesus Keep Me Near the Cross" reveals Fanny's desire that her entire trust should ever be in what the Lord Jesus accomplished at Calvary's cross. Each verse has the following chorus.

> In the cross, in the cross,
> Be my glory ever,
> Till my raptured soul shall find
> Rest beyond the river.[75]

---

[73] Crosby, "Rescue the Perishing," *Sacred Songs & Solos* 814.

[74] Lucille Travis, *The Blind Girl's Song* (Fearn: Christian Focus, 2013), 115-16.

"Tell Me the Story of Jesus" recounts the birth, temptations, public ministry, sorrows, cross, and resurrection of our Lord Jesus Christ. It was the theme song of the famous Radio Bible Class, founded by Dr. M. R. De Haan, which was heard by millions.

Fanny wrote "Hold Thou My Hand" in a period of personal discouragement. Normally a bright, optimistic person, such melancholy was unusual for her. Asking the Lord to hold her hand, she felt comforted and reassured. The hymn is credited to one of her many pseudonyms, Grace J. Frances. Susannah Spurgeon, the wife of the great Baptist preacher, found this hymn to be a particular comfort after her husband's death.

> Hold Thou my hand! So weak I am and helpless,
> I dare not take one step without Thy aid;
> Hold Thou my hand! For then, O loving Saviour,
> No dread of ill shall make my soul afraid.

> Hold Thou my hand! And closer, closer draw me
> To Thy dear self, my hope, my joy, my all;
> Hold Thou my hand! Lest haply I should wander,
> And, missing Thee, my trembling feet should fall.

> Hold Thou my hand! The way is dark before me,
> Without the sunlight of Thy face divine;

---

[75] Crosby, "Jesus Keep Me Near the Cross," *Christian Hymns,* 732.

But when by faith I catch its radiant glory,
What heights of joy, what rapturous songs are mine!

Hold Thou my hand! That when I reach the margin
Of that lone river Thou didst cross for me,
A heavenly light may flash along its waters,
And every wave like crystal bright shall be.[76]

One of Fanny's best known songs, "All the Way My Savior Leads Me," has been included in hundreds of hymnals. It illustrates how the Savior leads the Christian all the way through life, giving inward peace to comfort and grace to strengthen for every trial. Another gifted composer, Robert Lowry, composed the tune.

All the way my Saviour leads me:
What have I to ask beside?
Can I doubt His tender mercy,
Who through life has been my Guide?
Heavenly peace, divinest comfort,
Here by faith in Him to dwell!
For I know whate'er befall me,
Jesus doeth all things well.

---

[76] Crosby, "Hold Thou My Hand," *Alexander's Hymns No. 3*, 388.

All the way my Saviour leads me:
Cheers each winding path I tread,
Gives me grace for every trial,
Feeds me with the living bread.
Though my weary steps may falter,
And my soul athirst may be,
Gushing from the rock before me,
Lo! A spring of joy I see.

All the way my Saviour leads me;
O the fullness of His love!
Perfect rest to me is promised
In my Father's house above.
When my spirit, clothed, immortal,
Wings its flight to realms of day,
This my song through endless ages –
Jesus led me all the way.[77]

As with the work of Horatius Bonar, two of Fanny's hymns adhere to the strict definition given earlier. "To God Be the Glory," based on John 3:16, was frequently sung during Billy Graham's 1954 London Crusade. It became the theme hymn in the closing weeks and was repeated almost every night, due to its solid text and beautiful music—not to mention the hearty singing it inspired of the audience.

---

[77] Crosby, "All the Way My Savior Leads Me," *Christian Hymns*, 770.

To God be the glory, great things He has done;
So loved He the world that He gave us His Son,
Who yielded His life an atonement for sin
And opened the life gate that all may go in.
(chorus)
Praise the Lord! Praise the Lord! Let the earth hear His voice.
Praise the Lord! Praise the Lord! Let the people rejoice.
O come to the Father through Jesus the Son,
And give Him the glory, great things He has done.

O perfect redemption, the purchase of blood,
To every believer the promise of God;
The vilest offender who truly believes,
That moment from Jesus a pardon receives.
(chorus)

Great things He has taught us, great things He has done,
And great our rejoicing through Jesus the Son;
But purer, and higher, and greater will be
Our wonder, our rapture, when Jesus we see.
(chorus)[78]

The first verse of "Praise Him! Praise Him! Jesus Our Blessed Redeemer!" portrays Jesus as the Shepherd of His people. The

---

[78] Crosby, "To God Be the Glory," *Christian Hymns*, 137.

second tells how He laid down His life for sinners, and the
third celebrates His glorious and victorious resurrection.

Praise Him, praise Him! Jesus our blessed Redeemer;
Sing, O earth, His wonderful love proclaim!
Hail Him, hail Him! highest archangels in glory,
Strength and honour give to His holy Name.
Like a shepherd, Jesus will guard His children,
In His arms He carries them all day long;
O ye saints that dwell in the mountains of Zion,
Praise Him, Praise Him! ever in joyful song.

Praise Him! Praise Him! Jesus our blessed Redeemer;
For our sins He suffered and bled and died.
He, our Rock, our hope of eternal salvation,
Hail Him, hail Him! Jesus the crucified.
Loving Saviour, meekly enduring sorrow,
Crowned with thorns that cruelly pierced His brow;
Once for us rejected, despised, and forsaken,
Prince of glory, ever triumphant now.

Praise Him, praise Him! Jesus our blessed Redeemer;
Heavenly portals loud with hosannas ring!
Jesus, Saviour, reigneth for ever and ever,
Crown Him, crown Him! Prophet and Priest and King!
Death is vanquished, tell it with joy, ye faithful!

Where is now thy victory, boasting grave?

Jesus lives, no longer thy portals are cheerless;

Jesus lives, the mighty and strong to save.[79]

Although Fanny was blind, she greatly anticipated seeing her Savior when she got to Heaven. In Revelation 14:1-5, the apostle John records a vision of the Lamb of God on the heavenly Mount Zion. The redeemed are with Him. The harpists are playing their harps, and the redeemed are singing a new song that only they can truly sing. Likewise, "Some Day the Silver Cord Will Break" shows how Fanny looked forward to being with her Redeemer, seeing Him in all His beauty, and singing His praises forever.

Some day the silver cord will break,

And I no more as now shall sing;

But oh, the joy when I shall wake

Within the palace of the King!

(chorus)

And I shall see Him face to face,

And tell the story—Saved by grace;

And I shall see Him face to face,

And tell the story—Saved by grace.

---

[79] Crosby, "Praise Him! Praise Him! Jesus Our Blessed Redeemer!," *Christian Hymns*, 179.

Some day my earthly house will fall.
I cannot tell how soon 'twill be;
But this I know—my All in All
Has now a place in heaven for me.
(chorus)

Some day, when fades the golden sun
Beneath the rosy-tinted west,
My blessed Lord shall say, 'Well done!'
And I shall enter into rest.
(chorus)

Some day; till then I'll watch and wait—
My lamp all trimmed and burning bright—
That when my Saviour opes the gate,
My soul to Him may take its flight.
(chorus)[80]

This hymn has blessed many people. A friend of Fanny's once told her of a professed Christian who was struggling with overwhelming temptation and attended a church service, mainly to contemplate the situation while listening to the music. Upon hearing the words, "I shall see Him face to face,"[81] the person chose to live for God.

---

[80] Crosby, "Some Day the Silver Cord Will Break," *Sacred Songs & Solos*, 978.

[81] Ibid.

A former actress testified in a small Episcopal church in Pennsylvania that she had been indifferent to all religious influence. One afternoon, she set out to relax at a public park. As she passed along the street, unconscious of her surroundings, some singing caught her attention. Out of pure curiosity, she stopped to find that an Epworth League, a Methodist young adult association, was conducting services in the open air. As they sang "Saved by Grace," fond memories of childhood returned to her mind. As a result of the service, "she fell on her knees and asked the forgiveness of God."[82]

In addition to seeing her Savior, Fanny looked forward to seeing her grandmother, infant sister, daughter, and the many other Christian people she had loved and lost. "Oh, the Friends That Now Are Waiting" offers such comforting words that echo the truth of 1 Thessalonians 4:13-18.

How much they meant to my mother and me the day my father died! Our devotional reading for that day, entitled "A Great and Grand Reunion," suggested the Scripture portion; and the comment by Rev. Richard De Haan included some of the hymn.

> Oh, the friends that now are waiting,
> In the cloudless realms of day,
> Who are calling me to follow
> Where their steps have led the way.[83]

---

[82] Fanny Crosby, *Memories of Eighty Years* (London: Hodder & Stoughton, 1908), 158-159.

Fanny was thinking of her Christian loved ones in glory and felt that they, too, were looking forward to that day when we will all be together again. Whether we pass the vale of death or meet them in the air, there is going to be a great and grand reunion!

> I shall see them, I shall know them,
> I shall hear their song of love,
> And we'll all sing hallelujah
> In our Father's house above.[84]

---

[83] Crosby, "Oh, the Friends That Now Are Waiting," *Alexander's Hymns No. 3*, 393.

[84] Ibid.

CECIL FRANCES ALEXANDER
(1818-1895)

One of the most well-known hymns among non-church-going senior citizens in Great Britain is "There Is a Green Hill." They remember singing it at school assemblies when they were young. It is beautiful in its simplicity and clearly expresses the meaning of the cross. As a matter of fact, it was originally written for children, appearing in a book entitled *Hymns for Little Children* in 1848.

Cecil Frances Humphreys was born in Dublin in 1818 to John and Elizabeth Humphreys. Mr. Humphreys was a major in the British Army, and the family attended St. George's Church of Ireland until they moved to Wicklow seven years later. Fanny, as she was known, was brought up to be a churchgoing woman; however, her faith was real and personal, not mere creed orthodoxy.

When Fanny was sixteen or seventeen, two of her friends died, causing her to pause and affirm her belief in the afterlife and her trust in the Lord Jesus Christ as her Savior. This contemplation led her to love Him greatly, as she says in "There Is a Green Hill."

There is a green hill far away,
Outside a city wall,
Where the dear Lord was crucified,
Who died to save us all.

We may not know, we cannot tell,
What pains He had to bear;
But we believe it was for us
He hung and suffered there.

He died that we might be forgiven,
He died to make us good,
That we might go at last to heaven,
Saved by His precious blood.

There was no other good enough
To pay the price of sin;
He only could unlock the gate
Of heaven and let us in.

O dearly, dearly has He loved
And we must love Him too
And trust in His redeeming blood
And try His works to do.[85]

---

[85] Cecil Frances Alexander, "There Is a Green Hill." *Christian Hymns,* 261.

Trying to do good works does not contribute to one's salvation. However, it does show the genuineness of faith and love after conversion, and it is what God expects of believers (James 2:18; 1 John 3:18; Eph. 2:8-10; Luke 7:44-50).

Another of Fanny's hymns for children is the Christmas carol, "Once in Royal David's City." The fourth verse presents a paradox: how could the One Who was and is God and Lord of all ever be "weak and helpless"?[86] The answer is that He is both fully God and fully Man in one Person.

His true manhood developed in the normal way. "And the Child grew and became strong in spirit, filled with wisdom; and the grace of God was upon Him...Jesus increased in wisdom and stature, and in favor with God and men" (Luke 2:40, 52). At the same time, in Him dwelt "all the fullness of the Godhead bodily" (Col. 2:9), even when He was lying in the manger!

Once in Royal David's city
Stood a lowly cattle-shed,
Where a mother laid her Baby
In a manger for His bed.
Mary was that mother mild,
Jesus Christ her little Child.

He came down to earth from heaven
Who is God and Lord of all,

---

[86] Alexander, "Once in Royal David's City," *Christian Hymns*, 210.

And His shelter was a stable,
And His cradle was a stall.
With the poor and mean and lowly,
Lived on earth our Saviour holy.

And through all His wondrous childhood
He would honour and obey,
Love, and watch the lowly mother
In whose gentle arms He lay.
Christian children all must be
Mild, obedient, good as He.

For He is our childhood's pattern:
Day by day like us He grew;
He was little, weak, and helpless;
Tears and smiles like us He knew;
And He feeleth for our sadness,
And He shareth in our gladness.

And our eyes at last shall see Him,
Through His own redeeming love;
For that Child so dear and gentle
Is our Lord in heaven above;
And He leads His children on
To the place where He is gone.

Not in that poor lowly stable,
With the oxen standing by,
We shall see Him, but in heaven,
Set at God's right hand on high;
When like stars His children crowned
All in white shall wait around.[87]

The final line, "all in white shall wait around,"[88] does not sound dynamic, but *being* is more important than *doing*. The main thing is who is going to be in Heaven, not what they will do there. Referring to the blood-washed throng who have put their trust in Him, the Lord Jesus says, "They shall walk with Me in white" (Rev. 3:4). That prospect may not sound exciting until people remember with Whom they will be walking!

"All Things Bright and Beautiful" gives a lovely expression of delight in the wonders of God's creation, still visible in spite of the fall of Mankind.

All things bright and beautiful,
All creatures great and small,
All things wise and wonderful,
The Lord God made them all.

---

[87] Ibid.

[88] Ibid.

Each little flower that opens,
Each little bird that sings,
He made their glowing colours,
He made their tiny wings:
(chorus)

The purple-headed mountain,
The river running by,
The sunset, and the morning
That brightens up the sky:
(chorus)

The cold wind in the winter,
The pleasant summer sun,
The ripe fruits in the garden,
He made them, every one:
(chorus)

The tall trees in the greenwood,
The meadows where we play,
The rushes by the water
We gather every day:
(chorus)

He gave us eyes to see them,
And lips that we might tell

How great is God Almighty,
Who has made all things well:
(chorus)[89]

Fanny married William Alexander (a gentleman six years her junior) in 1850, two years after her *Hymns for Little Children* was published. Their married life began in County Tyrone, where he had recently been appointed the rector of a church. They "threw themselves into the work of the parish with enthusiasm," and "Fanny started to write hymns for adults rather than children."[90]

"Jesus Calls Us O'er the Tumult" calls Christians to give themselves wholeheartedly to following and serving the Lord Jesus, just as the apostles did (Matt. 4:18-22; Rom. 12:1-2).

Jesus calls us; o'er the tumult
Of our life's wild, restless sea,
Day by day His sweet voice soundeth,
Saying, "Christian, follow Me."

As of old apostles heard it
By the Galilean lake,
Turned from home and toil and kindred,
Leaving all for His dear sake.

[89] Alexander, "All Things Bright and Beautiful," *Christian Hymns* (Bridgend: Evangelical Movement of Wales, 1985), 850.

[90] Valerie Wallace, *Mrs. Alexander* (Dublin: Lilliput Press, 1995), 106, 110.

Jesus calls us from the worship
Of the vain world's golden store:
From each idol that would keep us,
Saying, "Christian, love Me more."

In our joys and in our sorrows,
Days of toil, and hours of ease,
Still He calls, in cares and pleasures,
"Christian, love Me more than these."

Jesus calls us—by Thy mercies,
Saviour, may we hear Thy call,
Give our hearts to Thy obedience,
Serve and love Thee best of all.[91]

Fanny Alexander died in 1895 at the age of seventy-seven. Her husband, William, then the bishop of Derry and Raphoe, officiated at the graveside and could not check his sobs as her earthly remains were laid to rest; but Fanny's soul had gone straight to Heaven, saved by the Lord Jesus Christ's precious blood, as it says in her immortal hymn, "There Is a Green Hill."

---

[91] Alexander, "Jesus Calls Us O'er the Tumult," *Golden Bells*, 467.

&LIZA &DMUNDS ⅎEWITT
(1851-1920)

Like Philip Bliss, Eliza was born in Pennsylvania. The second of six children, Eliza was a bright girl and obtained a teaching position after graduating from the Girls' High School in Philadelphia. A spinal injury cut her promising career short, however, and she was homebound for several years. The tragedy led her to write Sunday school literature and children's poems that caught the attention of composer and professor John Sweney, who requested she write pieces he could set to music. Her new chapter as a hymn writer began.

My own interest in Miss Hewitt stems from the fact that she wrote my all-time favorite hymn, "My Faith Has Found a Resting Place." I came across this hymn many years ago, and it goes right to the heart of my faith in the Lord Jesus Christ better than any other hymn I know. It is set to a melodious Norse air that was arranged by William James Kirkpatrick (1838-1921), also a resident of Philadelphia, who was friends with Professor Sweney.

> My faith has found a resting-place,
> Not in a form or creed;

I trust the Ever-living One,
His wounds for me shall plead.

(chorus)
I need no other argument,
I need no other plea,
It is enough that Jesus died,
And that He died for me.

Enough for me that Jesus saves,
This ends my fear and doubt;
A sinful soul I come to Him,
He'll never cast me out.
(chorus)

My heart is leaning on the Word,
The written Word of God,
Salvation by my Saviour's name,
Salvation through His blood.
(chorus)

My great Physician heals the sick,
The lost He came to save;
For me His precious blood He shed,
For me His life He gave.
(chorus)[92]

---

[92] Elizabeth Edmunds Hewitt, "My Faith Has Found a Resting Place," 291.

Some hymnals change the second line of the first verse to "from guilt my soul is freed,"[93] which alters the meaning somewhat. Perhaps editors wanted to avoid the impression that creeds and statements of faith are unimportant, but one need not suppose that was Miss Hewitt's intent.

Believing that certain things are true is important, but saving faith encompasses more than that. One must trust in the Lord Jesus Christ as personal Savior; as such, the second line of the first verse says something significant that should not be omitted. The hymn emphasizes that saving faith is based upon what the Lord Jesus Christ accomplished for us at Calvary and what God promises in Scripture. The second verse clearly has John 6:37 in mind: "All that the Father gives Me will come to Me, and the one who comes to Me I will by no means cast out." The third verse also emphasizes that saving faith is a thing of the heart and that it relies on the way of salvation set forth by the Word of God.

As for verse four, note well the personal emphasis. Martin Luther told Christians to "read therefore with great vehemency these words 'me' and 'for me,' that thou with sure faith mayest conceive and print this 'me' in thy heart, not doubting but that thou art of the number to whom this 'me' belongeth."[94] He was

---

[93] Hewitt, "My Faith Has Found a Resting Place," *Christian Hymns* (Bridgend: Evangelical Movement of Wales and Christian Hymns Committee, 2004), 623.

[94] Martin Luther, *Commentary on Galatians* (Grand Rapids: Kregel Publications, 1979), 96.

commenting on the words of Galatians 2:20, which say, "I live by faith in the Son of God, who loved me and gave Himself for me."

At one point, the treatment for Eliza's spinal injury required her to spend six months in a heavy body cast. When she was finally released from it, she was so grateful to go for a walk outside in the park that she wrote "Sunshine in My Soul," a lovely expression of what it means to be filled "with all joy and peace in believing" (Rom. 15:13). Professor John Sweney composed a melody to accompany the words. Eventually, Eliza's physical condition improved, and her increased mobility allowed her to take a more active part in the Lord's work. Serving as the superintendent of the primary department at Calvin Presbyterian Church, in particular, gave her great joy.

There is sunshine in my soul today,
More glorious and bright
Than glows in any earthly sky,
For Jesus is my Light.

(chorus)
Oh, there's sunshine, blessed sunshine,
When the peaceful, happy moments roll;
When Jesus shows His smiling face,
There is sunshine in my soul.

There is music in my soul today,

A carol to my King,

And Jesus, listening, can hear

The songs I cannot sing.

(chorus)

There is spring-time in my soul today;

For when the Lord is near,

The dove of peace sings in my heart,

The flowers of grace appear.

(chorus)

There is gladness in my soul today,

And hope, and praise, and love;

For blessings which He gives me now,

For joys laid up above.

(chorus)[95]

The most well-known of Eliza Hewitt's hymns in modern times could be "More About Jesus Would I Know." It speaks of her desire to "grow in grace, and in the knowledge of our Lord and Savior Jesus Christ" (2 Pet. 3:18). She had been saved by grace through faith in Him, and sunshine was in her soul. But she longed to know Him better and walk ever more closely with

---

[95] Hewitt, "Sunshine in My Soul," *Sacred Songs & Solos*, 872.

Him through life, as should every believer. Again, the original tune was by Professor John Sweney.

More about Jesus would I know,
More of His grace to other show,
More of His saving fullness see,
More of His love—who died for me.

(chorus)
More, more about Jesus,
More, more about Jesus,
More of His saving fulness see,
More of His love who died for me.

More about Jesus let me learn,
More of His holy will discern,
Spirit of God, my Teacher be,
Showing the things of Christ to me.
(chorus)

More about Jesus, in His Word,
Holding communion with my Lord,
Hearing His voice in every line,
Making each faithful saying mine.

(chorus)

More about Jesus, on His throne,

Riches in glory all His own,

More of His kingdom's sure increase,

More of His coming, Prince of Peace!

(chorus)[96]

In "I am Thinking Today of that Beautiful Land," Eliza speaks of the joy of not only being in that land but also having something of eternal value to offer her Lord and Savior in that glorious day, as described in 1 Corinthians 3:11-15 and 1 Thessalonians 2:19-20.

Unlike people who "linger shivering on the brink"[97] of Heaven, Eliza resembled the apostle Paul and all those believers who "rejoice in hope of the glory of God" (Rom. 5:2); "Sing the Wondrous Love of Jesus" demonstrates this attitude. She wrote it in collaboration with Emily D. Wilson, the wife of a Methodist district superintendent whom she met while attending a camp meeting in Ocean Grove, New Jersey. Eliza wrote the words; Emily composed the melody.

Sing the wondrous love of Jesus;

Sing His mercy and His grace;

In the mansions bright and blessed

He'll prepare for us a place.

---

[96] Hewitt, "More About Jesus Would I Know," *Christian Hymns,* 654.

[97] Watts, "There Is a Land of Pure Delight," *Christian Hymns,* 863.

(chorus)

When we all get to heaven,

What a day of rejoicing that will be!

When we all see Jesus,

We'll sing and shout the victory.

While we walk the pilgrim pathway,

Clouds will overspread the sky;

But when travelling days are over,

Not a shadow, not a sigh.

(chorus)

Let us, then, be true and faithful,

Trusting, serving every day;

Just one glimpse of Him in glory

Will the toils of life repay.

(chorus)

Onward to the prize before us!

Soon His beauty we'll behold;

Soon the pearly gates will open,

We shall tread the streets of gold.

(chorus)[98]

---

[98] Hewitt, "Sing the Wondrous Love of Jesus," *Alexander's Hymns No. 3*, 136.

The evening before he was crucified, the Lord Jesus told his disciples that he would soon be leaving them (John 13:33). When they heard this, sorrow filled their hearts and then, worse still, the Lord Jesus told Simon Peter that he would deny him three times (John 13:38). However, the Lord went straight on to say,

> Let not your heart be troubled; you believe in God, believe also in Me. In My Father's house are many mansions; if it were not so, I would have told you. I go to prepare a place for you. And if I go and prepare a place for you, I will come again and receive you to Myself; that where I am, there you may be also (14:1-3).

What comforting words! And not only to the disciples in the upper room, but also to every Christian. 'My Father's house' is heaven, the abode of God. (The Bible uses the word 'heaven' in three ways. The first heaven is what we call 'the earth's atmosphere', the second heaven is what we call 'outer space' and the third heaven is the abode of God. In 2 Corinthians 12:2-4, the apostle Paul speaks about being 'caught up to the third heaven', meaning that he was caught up into the very presence of God.) 'Many mansions' could also be translated 'many dwelling places' or 'many homes' (the same Greek word is translated 'home' in John 14:23). There are plenty of dwelling places in heaven for sinners. Heaven is the home of all who put their trust in the Lord Jesus Christ. He died for our sins at Calvary's cross, was buried, and rose again the third day (1 Corinthians 15:3-4). Then, after forty days, 'He was taken up' into heaven (Acts 1:1-3) to 'prepare a place' for us there. Because He, the Saviour who died for us, is there, we can be there too (1 Thessalonians 5:9-10).

The Christian life can be summed up in terms of faith, love and hope. For example, when the apostle Paul wrote to the Christians at Colosse, he said, 'we heard of your faith in Christ Jesus and of your love for all the saints; because of the hope which is laid up for you in heaven . . . ' (Colossians 1:3-5). They trusted in the Lord Jesus Christ as their Saviour, they loved God, they loved his people and they looked forward to 'the hope which is laid up for you in heaven'. So can every Christian![99]

> When we all get to Heaven,
> What a day of rejoicing that will be!
> When we all see Jesus,
> We'll sing and shout the victory![100]

---

[99] Currie, *What Happens When?: Answers to Questions for New Christians (Following Jesus)* (Leominster: Day One Publications, 2016), 16-18.

[100] Hewitt, "Sing the Wondrous Love of Jesus," *Alexander's Hymns No. 3*, 136.

&PILOGUE

I have sought to introduce readers to the great wealth of English hymnody, inherited from past generations. I believe we should sing the best of the modern spiritual songs, but we should not stop there.

Singing the great psalms and hymns of the past is important because it connects us with church history. The apostle Paul speaks about "the whole family in heaven and earth" (Eph. 3:15). As Christians, we are part of a great family, which is not only worldwide but also throughout time. Those believers who went before us comprise "so great a cloud of witnesses" (Heb. 12:1), who encourage us to "run with patience the race that is set before us" (Heb. 12:1). It is good for us to remember the example of the heroes of faith and to sing their songs as well. This is what the Apostles' Creed means by the communion of saints—our fellowship with those who have gone before.

Dr. Martyn Lloyd-Jones claimed that what evangelicals taught in his day on a particular subject was different from what evangelicals in earlier centuries taught; that thought prompted me to study church history. I decided to go right back to Martin Luther, the great Protestant Reformer. This exercise was a great blessing to me. Admittedly, the first biography of his life seemed as dull as ditch water, but then a friend loaned me a copy of *Here I Stand: A Life of Martin Luther* by Professor Roland Bainton. To me, the latter biography is as thrilling as the other is dull!

My point is that a connection with church history is important. We can achieve it both by reading church history and singing the great hymns of the past. Isaac Watts gives us the doctrines of grace expressed in beautiful poetry; Charles Wesley does likewise, helping us feel what the evangelical revival was like. The *Olney Hymns* of Newton and Cowper are simple and unpretentious, gracious, and full of love for the Lord Jesus. I believe that all of the ten great hymn writers featured in this book add something (and, of course, many others have besides these examples). In the words of John Newton, I conclude:

> Let us praise, and join the chorus
> Of the saints enthroned on high;
> Here they trusted Him before us,
> Now their praises fill the sky:
> "You have washed us with Your blood;
> You are worthy, Lamb of God."[101]

---

[101] John Newton, "Let Us Love, and Sing, and Wonder" *Christian Hymns*, 711.

APPENDIX
ALL PSALMS AND HYMNS MENTIONED WITH SUGGESTED TUNE

Century	Author	Title / First Line	Suggested Tune
4th	Ambrose of Milan	O Jesus, Lord of Heavenly Grace	Melcombe
Unknown	Unknown (Greek)	The King Shall Come When Morning Dawns	St. Stephen
12th	Bernard of Clairvaux	Jesus, Thou Joy of Loving Hearts	Maryton
12th	Bernard of Cluny	Jerusalem the Golden	Ewing
16th	Martin Luther	A Safe Stronghold Our God Is Still	Ein' Feste Burg

16th	Martin Luther	Come, Holy Spirit, God and Lord	Williams
16th	William Kethe	All People That on Earth Do Dwell	Old Hundredth
17th	George Herbert	Let All the World in Every Corner Sing	Luckington
17th	Joachim Neander	Praise to the Lord, the Almighty, the King of Creation	Lobe den Herren
17th	John Bunyan	Who Would True Valour See	Monks Gate
17th	Martin Rinkart	Now Thank We All Our God	Nun Danket
17th	Paul Gerhardt	O Sacred Head, Sore Wounded	Passion Chorale

17th	Samuel Crossman	My Song Is Love Unknown	Love Unknown
17th	Scottish Psalter	The Lord's My Shepherd	Crimond
17th	Thomas Ken	Glory to Thee, My God, This Night	Tallis' Canon
17th	Unknown (Latin)	O Come, All Ye Faithful	Adeste Fideles
18th	Isaac Watts	Alas! and Did My Saviour Bleed	Abney
18th	Isaac Watts	Come, Let Us Join Our Cheerful Songs	Nativity
18th	Isaac Watts	Give to Our God Immortal Praise	Galilee
18th	Isaac Watts	How Pleased and Blest Was I	Ascalon

18th	Isaac Watts	How Sad Our State by Nature Is!	Dundee
18th	Isaac Watts	I'll Praise My Maker While I've Breath	Monmouth
18th	Isaac Watts	Jesus Shall Reign Where'er the Sun	Rimington
18th	Isaac Watts	Join All the Glorious Names	Rhosymedre
18th	Isaac Watts	Not All the Blood of Beasts	Boylston
18th	Isaac Watts	Sweet Is the Work, My God, My King	Deep Harmony
18th	Isaac Watts	There Is a Land of Pure Delight	Beatitudo
18th	Isaac Watts	When I Survey the Wondrous Cross	Rockingham

18th	Charles Wesley	And Can It Be That I Should Gain?	Sagina
18th	Charles Wesley	Blessed Are They, Supremely Blest	Lasus
18th	Charles Wesley	Forth in Thy Name, O Lord, I Go	Angel's Song
18th	Charles Wesley	Hark the Herald Angels Sing	Mendelssohn
18th	Charles Wesley	Jesu, Lover of My Soul	Aberystwyth
18th	Charles Wesley	Jesus! The Name High Over All	Lydia
18th	Charles Wesley	O for a Thousand Tongues to Sing	Denfield
18th	Charles Wesley	O Love Divine! What Have You Done?	St Chrysostom

18th	Charles Wesley	O Thou Who Camest from Above	Wilton
18th	Charles Wesley	Soldiers of Christ, Arise	From Strength to Strength
18th	John Newton	Amazing Grace! How Sweet the Sound	Amazing Grace
18th	John Newton	Begone, Unbelief; my Saviour is Near	Houghton
18th	John Newton	Glorious Things of Thee are Spoken	Austria
18th	John Newton	How Sweet the Name of Jesus Sounds	St. Peter
18th	John Newton	Let Us Love, and Sing, and Wonder	All Saints

18th	John Newton	One There Is, Above All Others	Gounod
18th	John Newton	Quiet, Lord, My Froward Heart	Cassel
18th	John Newton	Though Troubles Assail and Dangers Affright	Houghton
18th	William Cowper	God Moves in a Mysterious Way	Dundee
18th	William Cowper	Hark, My Soul, It Is the Lord	St. Bees
18th	William Cowper	Sometimes a Light Surprises	Bentley
18th	William Cowper	There Is a Fountain Filled with Blood	Evan

18th	William Williams	Awake, My Soul, and Rise	Wirksworth
18th	William Williams	Guide Me, O Thou Great Jehovah	Cwm Rhondda
18th	William Williams	Jesus, Jesus All-Sufficient	Llwynbedw
18th	William Williams	The Enormous Load of Human Guilt	Lloyd
19th	Horatius Bonar	Heaven at Last!	St. Aubin
19th	Horatius Bonar	Fill Thou My Life, O Lord My God	St. Fulbert
19th	Horatius Bonar	Glory Be to God the Father	Regent Square
19th	Horatius Bonar	Help Me, My God, to Speak	St. Michael
19th	Horatius Bonar	I Hear the Words of Love	St. Michael

19th	Horatius Bonar	I Heard the Voice of Jesus Say	Kingsfold
19th	Horatius Bonar	No Blood, No Altar Now	Kelso
19th	Horatius Bonar	No, Not Despairingly Come I to Thee	St. Barnabas
19th	Horatius Bonar	Not What I Am, O Lord, but What Thou Art!	St. Agnes
19th	Horatius Bonar	Rejoice and Be Glad! The Redeemer Has Come	Thine the Glory
19th	Philip Bliss	Almost Persuaded Now to Believe	Same as Title
19th	Philip Bliss	Free from the Law, Oh, Happy Condition!	Same as Title

19th	Philip Bliss	Hallelujah! 'Tis Done.	'Tis the Promise of God
19th	Philip Bliss	Hold the Fort	Ho, My Comrades!
19th	Philip Bliss	I Am So Glad That Our Father in Heaven	Trinity Chapel
19th	Philip Bliss	I Will Sing of My Redeemer	My Redeemer
19th	Philip Bliss	Let the Lower Lights Be Burning	Same as Title
19th	Philip Bliss	Man of Sorrows	Gethsemane
19th	Philip Bliss	More Holiness Give Me	Same as Title
19th	Philip Bliss	One Offer of Salvation	Same as Title
19th	Philip Bliss	Standing by a Purpose True	Same as Title
19th	Philip Bliss	Whosoever Will	Same as Title

19th	Philip Bliss	Wonderful Words of Life	Words of Life
19th	Arthur Pierson	With Harps and With Vials	The New Song
19th	Horatio Spafford	When Peace, Like a River, Attendeth my Way	It Is Well
19th	James McGranahan	O What a Saviour That He Died for Me	Same as Title
19th	Fanny Crosby	A Few More Marchings Weary	Same as Title
19th	Fanny Crosby	All the Way My Saviour Leads Me	Same as Title
19th	Fanny Crosby	Hold Thou My Hand	Same as Title
19th	Fanny Crosby	I Am Thine, O Lord; I Have Heard Thy Voice	Grace Divine

19th	Fanny Crosby	Jesus, Keep Me Near the Cross	Near the Cross
19th	Fanny Crosby	Oh, the Friends That Now are Waiting	Same as Title
19th	Fanny Crosby	Pass Me Not, O Gentle Saviour	Same as Title
19th	Fanny Crosby	Praise Him, Praise Him! Jesus, Our Blessed Redeemer	Same as Title
19th	Fanny Crosby	Rescue the Perishing, Care for the Dying	Rescue
19th	Fanny Crosby	Some Day the Silver Cord Will Break	Saved by Grace
19th	Fanny Crosby	Tell Me the Story of Jesus	The Sweetest Story

19th	Fanny Crosby	To God Be the Glory	Same as Title
19th	C. Frances Alexander	All Things Bright and Beautiful	Same as Title
19th	C. Frances Alexander	Jesus Calls Us O'er the Tumult	St. Andrew
19th	C. Frances Alexander	Once in Royal David's City	Irby
19th	C. Frances Alexander	There Is a Green Hill	Horsley
19th	Eliza Hewitt	I Am Thinking Today of that Beautiful Land	Same as Title
19th	Eliza Hewitt	More About Jesus Would I Know	Same as Title
19th	Eliza Hewitt	My Faith Has Found a Resting Place	No Other Plea

19th	Eliza Hewitt	Sing the Wondrous Love of Jesus	Heaven
19th	Eliza Hewitt	There Is Sunshine in My Soul Today	Sunshine

BIBLIOGRAPHY

Alexander, Charles M. *Alexander's Hymns No. 3*. London: Marshall, Morgan and Scott, 1915.

Bliss, Philip. *Memoirs of Philip P. Bliss*. D.W. Whittle, ed. New York: A.S. Barnes and Company, 1877.

Broome, J.R. *Some Eighteenth Century Hymn Writers*. Stotfold: Gospel Standard Trust Publications, 2013

Cable, Mildred and Francesca French. *Through Jade Gate and Central Asia*. London: Hodder and Stoughton, 1943.

Christian Hymns. Bridgend: Evangelical Movement of Wales and Christian Hymns Committee, 1985.

Christian Hymns. Bridgend: Evangelical Movement of Wales and Christian Hymns Committee, 2004.

Crosby, Fanny J. *Memories of Eighty Years*. London: Hodder and Stoughton, 1908.

Currie, Peter. *Opening Up Romans*. Leominster: Day One Publications, 2022.

Currie, Peter. *What Happens When?: Answers to Questions for New Christians (Following Jesus)*. Leominster: Day One Publications, 2016.

Dallimore, Arnold. *A Heart Set Free: The Life of Charles Wesley*. Darlington: Evangelical Press, 1988.

Fountain, David G. *Isaac Watts Remembered: 1674-1748*. Southampton: Mayflower Christian Bookshop.

Gabriel, Charles Hutchinson. *The Singers and Their Songs*. Chicago: The Rodeheaver Company, 1916.

Gibb, Graham L. *Horatius Bonar and His Hymns*. Edinburgh: St. Catherine's Argyle Church, 1989.

Golden Bells. London: Scripture Union, 1925.

Horder, W. Garrett. *The Hymn Lover: An Account of the Rise and Growth of English Hymnody*. London: J. Curwen and Sons, 1889.

Houghton, Elsie. *Christian Hymn-writers*. Bridgend: Evangelical Press of Wales, 1982.

Luther, Martin. *Commentary on Galatians.* Grand Rapids: Kregel Publications, 1979.

Masters, Peter. *Men of Destiny.* London: The Wakeman Trust, 2017.

Psalms & Hymns of Reformed Worship. London: The Wakeman Trust, 1991.

Sacred Songs & Solos. London: Marshall, Morgan & Scott, 1977.

Travis, Lucille. *The Blind Girl's Song.* Fearn: Christian Focus, 2013.

Wallace, Valerie. *Mrs. Alexander.* Dublin: Lilliput Press, 1995.

About the Author

Peter Currie describes himself as only a sinner saved by grace. He spent twenty years working with an insurance company before becoming part of a team, producing computer software for insurance companies worldwide. During this time, he also served as a leader of a Crusader Bible class for boys. Then, for six years, he devoted himself to caring for his elderly mother. Now, he is very much involved in the work of Trinity Road Chapel in London, England, leading a team that ministers to the residents in nearby care homes and being part of the team that supports the church's missionaries.

Peter is the author of a number of published books, including a user guide for the Christian life, a short commentary on Paul's epistle to the Romans, two books about the promises of God, and an evangelistic booklet that explains simply and plainly what it means to be a Christian.

Ambassador International's mission is to magnify
the Lord Jesus Christ and promote His Gospel
through the written word.

We believe through the publication of Christian literature,
Jesus Christ and His Word will be exalted,
believers will be strengthened in their walk with Him,
and the lost will be directed to Jesus Christ
as the only way of salvation.

For more information about
AMBASSADOR INTERNATIONAL
please visit:
www.ambassador-international.com

Thank you for reading this book.

*Please consider leaving us a review on
your favorite retailer's website, Goodread, Bookbub,
or our website.*

ALSO AVAILABLE FROM
AMBASSADOR INTERNATIONAL

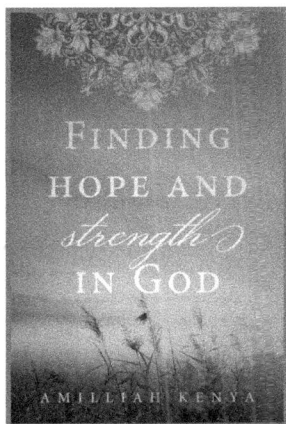

Finding Hope and Strength in God is a twelve-month devotional with different themes for each month focused on pointing you to your all-sufficient Savior, Who will give you strength and hope to face the day and to live a meaningful and fulfilling Christian life. Its practical approach to life will help you navigate real-life situations with tangible solutions to help you find meaning, hope, strength, and courage despite the tumultuous eventualities of life.

Throughout her years serving alongside her husband, who pastored Southside Baptist Church (now Fellowship Greenville) in Greenville, South Carolina, for over thirty years, Elizabeth Rice Handford has had the opportunity to touch many lives with her daily devotionals. In her new devotional, Fullness of Joy, take a dive into one hundred of Libby's devotionals, compiled from a look back through her writings and life experiences.

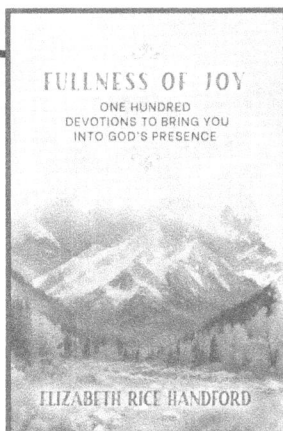

www.ingramcontent.com/pod-product-compliance
Lightning Source LLC
Chambersburg PA
CBHW071442090426
42737CB00011B/1752